Freelance Video Game Writing

Freelance Video Game Writing

The Life & Business of the Digital Mercenary for Hire

Toiya Kristen Finley, PhD

CRC Press
Taylor & Francis Group
Boca Raton London New York

CRC Press is an imprint of the
Taylor & Francis Group, an **informa** business

First Edition published 2022
by CRC Press
6000 Broken Sound Parkway NW, Suite 300, Boca Raton, FL 33487-2742

and by CRC Press
4 Park Square, Milton Park, Abingdon, Oxon, OX14 4RN

CRC Press is an imprint of Taylor & Francis Group, LLC

©2022 Toiya Kristen Finley, PhD

ISBN: 978-1-032-05904-4 (hbk)
ISBN: 978-1-032-05902-0 (pbk)
ISBN: 978-1-003-19977-9 (ebk)

DOI: 10.1201/9781003199779

Typeset in Minion
by Deanta Global Publishing Services, Chennai, India

*To everyone in the Rob Miles Networking Family Tree,
including my honorable networking grandfather, my networking
forefathers, my networking kids, and my networking grandkids.*

Y'all know who you are.

Contents

Glossary

Cooperative (co-op): A company established around a common need and where each of its members has an equal vote in company matters.

Daily rate: The amount paid per workday. Usually based on one's hourly rate.

Disregarded entity: A company that can be treated as a sole proprietorship and be reported on the individual member's tax returns.

Errors and omissions: A claim that a freelancer caused the injured party losses or damages due to the freelancer making a mistake in their work, the freelancer missing a deadline, or the work being inaccurate.

Fixed rate (also flat rate): The overall fee a freelancer will be paid. Can be paid in one lump sum or split into milestone payments.

Freelance platform: An online source where prospective clients post jobs and freelancers bid on them, or clients reach out directly to freelancers with profiles on the platform. Examples: Upwork, Fiverr, Freelancer, and Guru.

Hats: The variety of jobs individuals have on a project. If they're "wearing many hats," they could be writing, programming, providing art, etc.

Hourly rate: The amount paid per hour of work.

Indemnity clause: A clause in which any harm or damage, intentional or unintentional, caused to a party transfers from one contractual party to another.

Limited company (LC): A company in which the owner's or owners' assets are separate from the business entity. Also known as limited liability company (LLC) in certain territories.

Lowballing: Undervaluing a project by accepting and working for a much cheaper rate.

Milestone: An established point in the project when a freelancer will turn in a deliverable, a client will give feedback to the freelancer, or the freelancer will receive a payment.

Personal property tax: The amount individuals are taxed based on the appraised value of the equipment used in their business.

Prospective client: An individual identified as someone with whom a freelancer would like to consider engaging in a freelancer–client relationship.

Registered agent: A service that receives legal documentation on behalf of a business. Using a registered agent gives the business some privacy, as the public address for the business is that of the registered agent's.

Repeat client: A client who hires and works with a freelancer or independent contractor on more than one project.

Scope creep: Changes to and expansion of agreed-upon work responsibilities or overall project scope. Extra work that often goes unpaid.

Single-member LLC (SMLLC): A limited company owned by only one person.

Sole proprietorship: An unincorporated business where the business entity and the business owner are one and the same.

Up-front fee: A payment freelancers receive before any work begins. Usually a part of the agreed-upon overall fee for the project and often serves as a retainer.

Weekly rate: The amount paid per work week. Usually based on one's hourly rate and multiplied by the total number of work hours in the week.

Work-for-hire contract: An agreement between freelancer and client where all of the rights of the content produced by the freelancer will be retained by the client.

PART I

The Freelance Life

CHAPTER 1

Introduction

THERE ARE BOOKS OUT there that tell you how to make US$100,000 a year as a freelance writer.

This book is not one of them.

The game industry is super competitive. There's a lot of competition for freelancers, and you may strive to build a sustainable freelance business for several years before you get the kinds of jobs and rates that you want. On the other hand, someone who enters the industry at the exact same time as you may get a huge gig right away that lasts two years.

And, well, making US$100,000 a year may not be of interest to you. Maybe you just want to freelance on the side as a way to express yourself creatively.

So, why am I writing this book? All I've done is freelance. I'm a lone wolf or an outdoor cat that sometimes plays nicely with indoor cats (if you are more of the feline persuasion). Most of my adult life, my work has been done from my bedroom or den-turned-office in front of my laptop. In the time I've been freelancing, I only made one short trip to a studio. I don't even think I could be employed or work in an office at this time in my life. I wouldn't know what to do with myself. I *do* know that telecommuting as a writer, working digitally, is possible in this industry.

I originally planned this book pre-pandemic, long before COVID-19 shut down studios, and devs were suddenly forced to acclimate to working at home. The pandemic has shined a light on the importance of freelancers, years after friends and I had been advocating for studios to change their perspectives on freelance writers, trying to convince them that, yes,

DOI: 10.1201/9781003199779-2

we could be just as productive members of the team as anyone working in the office.

As I write this, we're almost two years into the pandemic. As awful as this time has been, a weird, fortuitous (it feels bizarre to even say that) thing has happened to some of my freelancer friends and me. Developers have been reaching out to us, and we suddenly have an abundance of queries and offers. I have not had any dry spells during this period, and I've had more work and financial stability than I did in the previous five years.

Why has this happened? I truly believe that telecommuting freelancers were uniquely positioned to work during the pandemic. We'd already figured out the work-at-home thing. With studios forced into being virtual, whether we were in-office or not was no longer an issue. And, hey, we proved that we *could* be valuable and productive members of the team.

When things return to whatever normal, it's my hope that freelancers will be just as valued as they are right now.

So, who is this book for? Whether you're a student or you've been in the industry 30 years, you can telecommute from home. It's for veteran freelancers, people who are looking to become freelancers out of curiosity or necessity, and developers who might be interested in working with freelancers, or who would like to strengthen their collaborative relationships with freelancers.

(I want to note that I'm using the term "freelancer" instead of "independent contractor" deliberately because this book is more about finding and working on more than one gig at once, while contractors are more likely to work with the same clients for longer periods of time. Much of the advice *does* also apply to contracting, though.)

Freelance Video Game Writing: The Life & Business of the Digital Mercenary for Hire is separated into two parts. Part I is a reflection on my own journey into freelancing and the importance of having good people (i.e., a network) around you. It was my journey and the people in my network who informed much of what is in this book.

The second part is the practical side of freelancing. Freelancing is a *business*, and we'll explore how to set up that business, maintain it, and build lasting relationships with clients.

All of this is from the point of view of a narrative designer and game writer because that's what I am, but there's hopefully plenty in here for all freelancers and the freelance curious, no matter your discipline in games.

Each chapter in Part II has an exercise or two (or three). The exercises are to help you think about the chapter's content and how you can directly apply it to your business. You may already be using some of the techniques in these exercises, so they may encourage you to re-evaluate an aspect of your business or rethink your practices and how you apply them.

Most chapters in Part II also have at least one interview from someone in my networking community. Every one of them is fantastically smart and thoughtful. Since freelancing can be so personal, I don't want my voice to be the only perspective you get. (And you should hear from someone who hires freelancers!) Someone else may have an insight or experience that jibes more with who you are and what you do.

It's been my experience that freelancers don't have a lot of spaces to talk shop about their experiences in the industry. I hope this book can shed light on what we do and open up more dialogue.

—TKF

CHAPTER 2

There's No One Path… and Here's Mine

THE VERY BEGINNING OF THE STORY…

Hang around game developers long enough, and you'll realize there's no one way to get into the industry. The number of developer origin stories is as unique as the number of developers.

The same is true of freelancers. People become freelancers or independent contractors for all sorts of reasons.

I became a freelancer by accident. The truth is I was a freelancer at heart long before I realized I could be self-employed or seek out and accept the jobs and clients I wanted. My training as a freelancer started when I was 14 years old. In a three-year period, I had written a couple of novels, and I was determined to publish them. I read (very wrong) advice that in order to sell a novel I would have to publish some short stories first.

Now, I was not a short story writer. I didn't understand how you could condense someone's life into ten pages. But I started writing short stories, anyway—anything to sell my novels. (As you can imagine, my first attempts at stories read like I was trying to get a novel squished into ten pages.) I did plenty of research on how to submit stories. Back then, you needed piles of 10 × 12 envelopes, stacks of 8 × 11 white sheets of paper, lots of toner cartridges, rolls of stamps, and letter-sized envelopes for the SASE.[1] Through research, I became an expert on short fiction markets and targeted the ones that I really wanted to appear in, imagining my name on the covers.

DOI: 10.1201/9781003199779-3

That was part of my training as a freelancer. Freelancers get to decide with whom they want to work. (The very concept of the freelancer developed from the idea that medieval mercenaries fought for the individual or nation who gave them the most money.)[2] Once the stories went off in the mail, I learned—and endured—a most important aspect of the freelance life. Submitting your work, especially as an inexperienced writer, is an exercise in agony and perpetual waiting. When you get that response back, most likely a rejection, that cycle starts all over again. I sent out story, after story, after story, *after story*. A short wait was two months. The agonizing waits? Six months…A year…And when I *did* get a response, it was a form letter in that SASE. Sometimes, when the editors knew I was a young writer, they'd write me a note of encouragement. Knowing how many stories editors have to wade through and how draining it is to read through them, I appreciate the time they took to send feedback a lot more now than I did then.

Just like writers who get rejections after what feels like an endless wait, freelancers send off queries and applications. They may never get a response. They may get a form rejection with no explanation as to why they were rejected. And when they do get referrals, or the prospective client[3] comes directly to them to request a submission, they still may end up rejected.

Freelancers, like writers, have to develop a granite-hard callous. I don't know a writer or a freelancer who grew that callous quickly. Some still haven't after many years. And even after you develop the callous, it doesn't mean you won't feel the rejection.

While I was writing, submitting, getting hundreds of rejections, and slowly gaining some acceptances in the mix, I learned another valuable lesson that would serve me well as a freelancer: Always be professional. A misplaced comma or a typo in the cover letter was a harbinger of what was to come in the manuscript. These mechanical errors would say a lot about the writer's overall skill, from the handle (or lack thereof) on grammar to style, to plot development. (I would later find out that mechanical skills were a sure telltale sign as a composition instructor, too.) Realizing editors were watching for writing errors like the Eye of Sauron made me proofread carefully, and I always wanted to strike the right tone in my cover letters. (I was probably too obsessive in that regard, reading them over and over and over and over again to make sure I didn't offend anyone.)

Professionalism easily separated great writers from those who, quite honestly, weren't as skilled at storytelling as they thought or weren't taking the time to make their stories as good as they could be. Freelancers who always act with professionalism appear more serious and trustworthy than those who don't. Well-written cover letters and well-formatted and structured docs make a greater impression than those samples that aren't. And if you're a personable yet professional communicator, you're someone prospective clients are more likely to trust with their projects and money.

I was a professional student for eight years, still submitting my work, which now included creative nonfiction and academic articles. I'd become an editor while I was in school, interning at Owl Books at Henry Holt & Company, being a part of editorial boards of literary journals at New York University and Iowa State, and founding my own journal at Binghamton University. And I was a teaching assistant as a master's student and a writing center tutor while I was getting my master's and PhD. I was picking up the skills I would use as a developmental editor, copyeditor, and proofreader.

Once I graduated, I just never got an employed job.

To be fair, I didn't *look* for one, either. I was selling stories, editing other people's stories, and doing the occasional writing job for someone else. I was freelancing without applying the label to myself. During this time, something I found that was imperative to me was that I had plenty of time to work on my own stuff, whether that was short stories or novels. I had the freedom of deciding what I would be doing throughout my day, when I wanted to work, and when I wanted to write—or do nothing at all. In my mind, rightly or wrongly, being employed would mean losing that freedom.

Eventually, I found what I thought was a stable, part-time contract—teaching online for ITT Technical Institute.[4]

A MUNDANE REVELATION

Let me back up a few years, back to when I was still pursuing my PhD at Binghamton University.

There were brief moments as a freshman that I actually found time to play games. But studying, an internship, and my own writing took over. I was disconnected from video games for a few years. I'd *always* played games. I remember taking a special trip to the department store with my father to buy an Atari 2600 when I was five years old. It was a few days after my cousins visited from Atlanta and I played *Pac-Man* on a cocktail arcade machine at Pizza Hut. After that, there were *always* video games and at least two consoles around. But once I went off to school, I missed an entire console generation. I didn't know what games were being hyped. I didn't know which studios and developers were reaching rock star (pun intended) status. Games were out of my life.

But they hadn't left my imagination. There were characters and scenarios running around in my head that I realized were perfect for a game. And, finally, I got an Xbox and a copy of *Shenmue II* while I was at Binghamton. Its sprawling open world and life-simulation elements sparked something in me. Suddenly, I was playing the evidence that ideas I had for games were entirely plausible. Even though I was a storyteller, even though I grew up as a gamer, I'd never considered working in games as something I could *do*.

Looking back at what I know now, I think I was not unlike a lot of marginalized people who love games and have amazing careers in the industry. When I was younger, there weren't game development programs. I had no friends who worked in games, and I was not connected to that community in any way. Nowadays, marginalized people don't have access to game development because *we don't know we* could *have access to game development*. Our parents and elders don't know these opportunities are there for us, our guidance counselors and teachers don't know, and we most likely don't live near game hubs where we might hear about studios and publishers. I will cover why this has to change in Chapter 15, "Some Final Thoughts."

Honestly, I knew nothing about the game industry. I mean, my knowledge was laughably less than basic. Beyond having an understanding that someone programmed the games (hey, I had a coding class in middle school), I had no idea about all of the roles and disciplines that could make up a team. I couldn't tell you the difference between AAA developers and publishers; small indie teams; or that one developer who did all of the programming, art, design, and writing themselves. All I *did* know is that I was good at writing, I wanted to write for games, and I was pretty sure I could write for them.

I was also pretty good at Google searches. Years of being a professional student honed those skills. I was ignorant of how to find game gigs but, thankfully, fell back on my knowledge of how to find writing and editing work. So, I typed in that search field, "game writing job."

Yeah, that's all I did.

And I got a hit, too! On Craigslist, of all places. A small indie start-up called Black Chicken Studios was looking for lore writers. If I try to do this now, I can't duplicate this experience. "Game writing job" now brings up salaried work on sites like Zip Recruiter, SimplyHired, and Indeed, and there are hits about what game writing is and what it entails, and how to find game writing jobs. But I've never been able to bring up a singular hit for freelance gigs like that first one I found. That's why, as freelancers, we shouldn't be unkind to ourselves, wondering why we can't get the same opportunities as friends and acquaintances. If you ask ten people how they got into the game industry or how they got the job they're on right now, you're going to get ten different stories. Every developer's history in games is deeply individual and unique to the opportunities that opened up to them at *just the right moment*. Your experiences and opportunities might be similar, but they'll never be the same as anyone else's. Take that from someone who can't duplicate her own experience of finding her first gig the first time she ever did a search for a game writing job and found the perfect hit on Google's first page.

That gig I found was specifically for lore writing. Sounded interesting… because I had no idea what a lore writer did. (Yes, I know, I had been writing fantasy and science fiction for all of my life, and still didn't intuit this.) When I visualized "game writing," what I was doing was thinking about "game design." (I didn't know what game design was, either. Remember, I knew absolutely nothing about the industry.) I assumed the game writer "wrote out" what the game was about and how to play it.

But lore writing was something I had been doing almost all of my life. Having no experience in the industry, I still had the tools and background experience to be a good game writer.

THE LEAN YEARS

About five years had passed from the time I realized I had some pretty good ideas for video games to the time I actually started searching for my first game writing gig. What took so long? Well, like I said, I was completely disconnected from the industry, and I probably had the (unconscious) perspective that only programmers made games. Plus, by the time I graduated from Binghamton, I was just trying to find work without having to be gainfully employed…*and* keep writing.

I landed as an adjunct teaching intro-level composition at ITT Technical Institute a few months later. ITT turned out to be…problematic, to put it lightly. Long story short, it engaged in a number of shady business practices that devastated students financially and resulted in sanctions from the US Department of Education. While I was unaware of this at the time, I felt its effects. "It rots from the head" is a saying for a reason.

I had been a TA at the master's level and taught composition at Iowa State University. I also worked with students at Binghamton's Writing Center. Teaching online seemed a natural fit. And this wasn't as complicated as my job at Iowa State. I didn't have to design the course or come up with lesson plans. All I had to do was understand what the students were learning each week, grade their assignments in a timely manner, and be available to them during online office hours. I was used to students hating composition courses. They were forced to take composition as a requirement, but they were anxious to take courses toward their majors. At Iowa State, reading about writing and writing essays whose subject matter they cared nothing about left them disinterested in the materials I worked hours to prepare for them, and sometimes their hostility for the course ended up aimed at me. Annoying? Frustrating? Sure, especially when I understood how relevant writing and communication were going to be in whatever they did in their future careers, and I couldn't get that through to them. But dealing with disinterested students was part of the job.

On the other hand, working (and I might even say "working") with ITT's students was a completely different and vicious beast. I had quite a few students who were a year or a couple of years older than me when I taught at Iowa State (something I was sure they never discovered). However, all of my ITT students were 10-20 years older than me. Their hostility and disinterest toward the material was dialed up to eleventy, and not only did they not care, but they also decided the best way to get through the course was to plagiarize all of their assignments. I do not exaggerate when I say that in one of my course sections, all but maybe one or two students plagiarized their work. Most of my time wasn't spent grading. I was tracking down the plagiarized sources. Even worse, this seemed to be common in many of the online courses. It was so rampant that ITT established a policy that if instructors did not discover an assignment was plagiarized when a student turned it in, they could not report the violation later. I suppose that when you're faced with losing lots and lots of money because you might have to kick cheating students out of school, your only recourse is to let them cheat. To make things worse, in the two years I taught there, I had one student who was genuinely interested in the course and met with me periodically to improve her writing.

A year into teaching at ITT, I wondered why I felt out of sorts. I was filled with this malaise that made no sense to me, and I couldn't figure out its source. That's when I realized that it had been over a year since I had worked on anything of my own. I mean I had not written anything in a notebook or a word processor since I started working with ITT. Forget about actually writing any stories. I had not even written a single note or brainstormed or outlined. My one saving grace is that because of the way my brain works with my writing process, I was still visualizing stories in my head. I don't know what I would have been like mentally if not for that.

I was burnt out long before I became familiar with the concept. This online adjunct position was draining me of my physical and mental energy. I was miserable and didn't realize it. My time was consumed with dealing with students and venting to close family and a program director at ITT. As it turned out, I was the only one *he* could vent to about the oppressive environment he was working in at the home office. I was so buried under ITT's toxic mix that I literally didn't have the capacity to even consider the possibility that I could be doing something else. Nor did I have the time or energy to look.

That First Big Gig

I had to go back and look at my CV to recreate my professional time line to write this chapter. It's amusing to see how I used to think of myself. After I left ITT, I started referring to myself as an "independent" writer and editor. It still hadn't clicked for me that I was freelancing. And that's probably because I wasn't around other people who used the term. Honestly, I don't remember why I was calling myself independent. I probably looked at some online résumés and adopted their language.

Two years after I left ITT, I had my first major break, and I wasn't looking for it. Freelance long enough (or hang around freelancers long enough), and you'll be a part of a lot of "right place, right time" circumstances. In this case, it wasn't me who was in the right place. It was my mother. A school psychologist, she was attending a conference in town and met the CEO of a start-up for kids. His goal was providing to schools a supplemental reading program for nonreaders and children having trouble reading. While my mother was networking with him, she mentioned I was a writer. I had a phone conversation with him later that afternoon.

It wasn't a week later that I had my first major freelancing job, and my title was "Head Writer."

Twenty hours a week for $50 an hour, I was planning, researching, and writing short e-books to get kids interested in reading. I had almost full creative freedom to write whatever I wanted, and I drew on my skills as a fiction and nonfiction writer and researcher. I created a couple of series, wrote a lot of fiction one-offs, wrote celebrity biographies, and researched cool science stuff like facts about seals and ants. I connected with my client once a week to catch them up on what I was doing, and then I went back to doing pretty much whatever I wanted.

This job was so important to me for a few major reasons. For the first time in my life, I had some real financial stability. I wasn't pressed to find work, and I had plenty of time to write for myself. Equally important was that I started to develop an internal clock for how long it took me to plan, research, and write these short e-books (similar to the internal clock I developed for writing short stories and operating under submissions deadlines). I could now guess how long a task would take me, and I was usually correct.

Around the same time I got this job, I started wondering if I should pursue writing for games, several years after playing *Shenmue II*. It finally dawned on me that *someone* was doing the writing (even if I was confused about what "writing" meant). I liked games. I was good at writing. Why couldn't one of those game writers be me? The only question for me was, "Is this the right time in my life?" I discussed it with my mother and a close friend and mentor, and they made it clear to me that there was no reason why I *shouldn't*.[5] They were right. When I decided to write for games, I found that gig with Black Chicken pretty quickly.

The Great GDC Adventure

There's a now-defunct online community for speculative fiction writers that I used to frequent. One of my friends there ran his own game studio. I asked him how I could become a game writer. His response was simple:

"Well, if you're really serious about writing for games, you should go to GDC."

That was the first time I had ever heard of GDC, or Game Developers Conference, the most important meeting of game developers every year. I had absolutely no idea what to expect, but I was not going to turn down the advice of a successful industry veteran. I was not anticipating GDC to be so expensive, however. Not only were conference badges pricy, but

I also had to fly out to San Francisco and stay there for a week. Going to GDC was an investment in my business and future.

My first year, I bought the cheapest pass. I didn't get access to any talks or roundtables, but I could go to the Expo Hall and talk with recruiters and HR types. Large and small studios were looking to hire, and I was pitching myself as a telecommuting game writer.

"We don't have any writer positions open."

"We use a firm to hire all of our writers."

"Uh, I don't know anything about hiring writers."

I had slammed into a wall. Where were all the people who needed writers? I mean, there was a space set up for all of the companies hiring devs. Shouldn't at least *one* of them be looking for writing help? I'm not sure how seriously any of them took me. They were looking to fill salaried positions. They weren't hiring freelancers. They weren't hiring writers. I was a misfit among all of the students who were about to graduate. *They* were getting called back for meetings and being hired on the spot.

Something that certainly didn't help was that I brought 50 copies of my eight-page CV to hand out. I stuffed them into a plastic accordion folder I carried around under my arm. I immediately knew I had labeled myself as the oddball in the room when I saw that everyone else had a one-sheet résumé—and no accordion folder. People politely took copies of my CV, but it was clear they were thinking, "Hell am I supposed to do with this?" Only one woman told me, "I'm going to hold on to your CV," because her studio often hired freelancers. (I finally found one! Although I didn't hear from her again.)

(A side note: A friend of mine took my CV to HR at his studio. Someone there gave my CV a once over and said, "Why does she want to work in games?" I mean, my CV had a lot of fiction writing on it and science fiction and fantasy and horror. Did all of the academic stuff somehow cancel out a reason why I *wouldn't* want to work in games?

Dear HR People and Anyone Responsible for Hiring:

If individuals tell you they want a job in a specific discipline or industry, please believe them. Do you think they're making it up for fun?

The greatest thing that happened to me at that first GDC was that I started to build my network. While I didn't have access to most of the conference, the after-parties were free. I met now lifelong friends at the first party I stepped into. They taught me a lot about networking at professional game conferences and how to approach new people.

Hey, There's a Writing Community!

My second GDC the very next year, I bought the all-access badge. It was expensive, but I realized I needed to be exposed to many more people. I was going to have to find the prospective clients who would actively be hiring writers. Plus, as someone who was working on her first game, I still knew very little about game development. I wanted access to GDC's content. Let me quickly note that I'm not advocating for freelancers to spend over a thousand dollars to get into conferences. Not everyone is able to do this, and there are other avenues to finding people who will become important parts of your network. If you have the means and you think it will be to your benefit, go to these more expensive events when you can.

The schedule didn't reveal many narrative-oriented sessions. There was, however, a roundtable for writers. I walked into a GDC tradition. Richard Dansky ran the Game Narrative Roundtable as a community where writers could share their best practices and commiserate. I sat there in silence for the full hour, simply amazed. *I had found my people.*

The only conversation I remember from that session was about barks.

I had no idea what they were talking about.

But that was *okay.* I got the gist of most of the conversation through context. More importantly, I realized my thoughts about narrative design and game design were instinctually correct. I could figure it out and do this thing, learning on the Black Chicken job.

But You Can't Live There…

I met very few freelancers during my first few years at GDC. When I introduced myself as wanting to telecommute, there was a notable refrain to the advice I was getting:

"To really be successful, you're going to have to move to a hub."

Ya know, one of the most expensive cities on the planet? Seattle…San Francisco…I could also move to Texas, if I wanted. Studios weren't hiring telecommuters. They wanted freelancers in the office with the rest of the team.

Lone wolves can't work in this industry. Stop being feral, outdoor cat, and learn to live inside.

Everyone who told me this was trying to be helpful. They wanted me to find work. They wanted me to be successful, but an indescribable dread washed over me every time I heard this. Moving—just to have the chance to find work—meant uprooting my life. It meant moving away from my family, my community, my physical and emotional safety nets. "Move to a city where they make lots of games!" was not as comforting as people probably thought.

I'm also hardheaded. If you tell me I can't do something, I'm going to prove you wrong, *especially* if I'm already doing the thing you're telling me I can't do. I knew telecommuting was possible. I knew how easy it was to communicate and work with clients across multiple time zones. Is it harder for team members in-office to work with telecommuters who aren't writers? I have no idea. But as far as my lived experience dictated to me, there was no good reason I could not telecommute as a game writer.

Finding the telecommuting game writing jobs would prove to be my biggest problem early on.

The First Big Loss

My first major freelancing gig ended after a little under a year. The reading program wasn't selling, and my client could no longer afford me. I loved that job for being my first major opportunity and the freedom it brought me. But I wasn't crushed when they had to let me go. I think it was because I had other work at the same time, and I now knew that my prospects as a game writer were good. I had a new avenue open to me.

(Kind of amazing how when your mental outlook changes, your imagination is free to pursue what you would consider impossible (or not consider at all) when you're burnt out.)

I was still working with Black Chicken, but losing my Head Writer position punched a major hole in my financial stability, and I needed to find other gigs to replace that loss. It was back to the grind of online searching for work. I went to websites like Mediabistro and Freelance Writing Jobs every day. I found small projects here and there, but nothing that was sustainable.

One of my searches led me to a freelance platform called Elance. Now defunct, Elance merged with oDesk to become Upwork. If you're familiar with Fiverr or Freelancer, Elance was somewhat similar. It was a way for freelancers and prospective clients to find each other. Prospective clients would post jobs. They would either invite freelancers to bid on those jobs, or they would make them public, where any freelancer could bid on them.

I learned a lot from veteran freelancers (including the term "prospective client"), lurking on the discussion forums. Freelancers on the site lowballed, and most clients offered to pay ridiculously low rates, which most freelancers gladly accepted. The veterans I paid attention to were successful outside of Elance and were able to ask for and receive professional rates on the site. Some of the advice that stuck with me was to establish your professional rates by taking on smaller jobs. For example, the best rate I got on the site was $110/hour for a game design document. It was a smaller project that took ten hours. The other important piece of advice was to find a niche and present yourself as an expert in it.

While there were plenty of writing and editing jobs posted, there was way too much competition from other freelancers who had longer histories on the site and who would literally work for pennies on the dollar. (I did win a couple of interesting and fulfilling writing projects because of my personal experience and educational background.) There weren't many game writing jobs, but they're the ones I most aggressively pursued.

Again, I found that I had a lot of freedom on most of these projects. The majority of my clients were making their first game. While they had a vague idea for the game, they leaned on me to come up with the game design and narrative design. Yes, I was doing the jobs of game designer, narrative designer, and game writer. This was *great* experience. However, I would later realize that I was making too little for the amount and complexity of the work, when I thought I was doing pretty good. I wanted to make more, but I was at a loss as to how to find those jobs.

Beyond the rates, what soured me on Elance were the types of clients and freelancers that took over the site a couple of years after I started using it. One of my clients tried to scam me out of payment (please see Chapter 14, "Please Learn from My Ignorance," for that story). The number of freelancers who flooded Elance, willing to work for almost nothing, made it impossible for me to find work. Eventually, Elance shut down. I had no real desire to be active on its revamped merger, Upwork.

You might wonder why I titled this section "The Lean Years," when it wasn't all bad. I had a great job that taught me a lot. I found my first game writing job in the easiest way possible and became a game designer and developed narrative design skills on that project. And while I had smaller projects, I was getting a self-taught education in game development as I had the freedom to implement a lot of my ideas into design and gameplay features.

"Lean" is certainly a matter of perspective. They *felt* lean to me. They were financially lean. They were lean as far as opportunities went, and the smaller, cheaper jobs were teaching me the hard lesson that I could have been earning more for the work I was doing.

IS A FREELANCE PLATFORM RIGHT FOR YOU?

Current freelance platforms include Fiverr, Freelancer, Guru, and Upwork. I won't tell you *not* to join a freelance site. However, protecting yourself is an important freelance skill, and knowing exactly how these freelance sites operate and the types of opportunities/lack of opportunities is part of that.

You might think I'm over exaggerating the need for caution, but I've been an editor at several literary journals. I interned at a major publishing company. I've also been a composition teacher. I know that people do not follow instructions or read guidelines. Not following instructions on a freelance website can get your account deactivated, get you scammed out of your money, or worse. People skim over websites' Terms of Service (ToS) or ignore them completely all of the time, but you certainly can't do that in this case. If you violate the ToS, you could be banned. For instance, Elance did not allow clients to ask for free sample work, and it didn't allow freelancers to do free sample work. If clients wanted samples, they had to pay for them. However, clients asked for free work, and they got it all of the time.

Prospective clients post their jobs, and they'll usually indicate a budget range they're willing to pay. You can always ask for more. Great freelancers often get above the prospective client's initial budget range. You bid for the job by sending in a proposal and telling the clients what your fee would be and how long it would take. Some of these sites allow communication with the client on or offsite, and they may allow turning in your work on or offsite. On other sites, all work must be turned in onsite.

Freelance websites also have their own governing independent contractor agreements. You need to know if you can use your own contract instead of the website's. You need to know where your contract should be posted. You need to know how jobs are awarded. I've seen freelancers wander into the forums saying they've completed the job, but the client hasn't paid them. How do they get paid? Well, as it turns out, they were never awarded the job. You have to be awarded jobs to be paid through the website's platform. Also, some of these websites will not take kindly to freelancers who accept payments off the platform. They get a percentage of your earnings. Getting paid offsite robs them of their money.

At least one of these websites has guaranteed protections for payment, *but* you need to make sure that you're following their rules, so those protections are in place. One of those protections might actually violate any nondisclosure agreements you're under.

In other words, RESEARCH, RESEARCH, RESEARCH. Look to see if these sites have jobs you're interested in or that fit your skills. Read everything you can about how these sites operate. Watch and read all of their tutorials. Understand how the site works better than new clients coming onto the site. (And understand it better than some of the customer support reps, but that's another story.)

P.S. A lot of people say they're looking for a game designer when they mean they really need a programmer or artist. And sometimes they actually *do* need a game designer. If you're going to use these sites, look over posts for game designers, even if you're not a game designer, just in case.

 FREELANCE WEBSITE CHECKLIST

- Read the Terms of Service (ToS).
- Read the contract agreements.
- Know how to add your own agreements, so they're legally binding.
- Know how jobs are awarded.
- Find out how freelancers are paid through the platform.
- Review the types of jobs posted.

THE TELECOMMUTING EXPERT

I took the "have a niche" mentality from Elance to my networking community. I became known as a telecommuting freelancer, and I was getting more projects through direct referrals. In 2014, when I was asked to speak at East Coast Game Conference, I talked about freelancing in an online environment. I tend to take on certain subjects after getting frustrated that no one else has. I knew there were other freelancers in the industry, but we were disconnected. We didn't have a support system to share stories or best practices. Furthermore, while developers were becoming more comfortable working with telecommuting freelancers, devs looking for work had no idea how to freelance successfully. You can't get a job if you don't know it's there for you.

At the same time, there was a shift in the industry. Veteran developers were being let go from their permanent jobs. My friends were losing their salaried positions. At GDC after hours, I was now sharing everything I knew about setting up a freelance business or giving pointers on how my friends might go about finding gigs. Several times a night, I had people walk up to me and say, "I was told I needed to come talk to you about freelancing."

Six years after I got the advice to pack up everything and move to a gaming hub, I gave a lecture at GDC on how to be a telecommuting freelancer.

It's now six years after that talk. I've co-moderated several roundtables at GDC for freelancers. I'm writing this book, and the unthinkable[6] happened during the COVID-19 pandemic: I made more money than I ever had. I've always had a weird relationship with money. It's not that I horde it—but the thought of "What if I don't make more money?" would loom over me. I couldn't spend money if I wasn't going to make more money. I would literally have the money I needed to pay a bill, but I would still be anxious about losing that money. I think I developed this mindset during my lean years. Most of what I earned went toward travel for conferences and paying off my student loans and other bills. Now, all of a sudden—during a pandemic, no less—I had enough in my account to actually pay freelancers to work on my own game project. Still feels weird, man. Good, but weird.

It took me almost 20 years of freelancing to be *comfortable*, to get to the place where I didn't have to worry if I had no work for several months. For some, it happens a lot faster. For others, it doesn't work out because freelancing isn't right for them—and that's okay.

Like I said, everybody's journey is different. Mine helped shape the insights in this book. I hope you can integrate some of them into your own business.

NOTES

1. The abbreviation for "Self-Addressed Stamped Envelope," the thing you had to include with your submission to get a response back from the editor. I'm still not sure how to pronounce this after all these years. *SAY-zee? ESS-AY-ESS-EE?*
2. An independent (*free*) individual with a weapon (*lancer*). "The Surprising History of 'Freelance,'" Merriam-Webster, accessed January 13, 2022, https://www.merriam-webster.com/words-at-play/freelance-origin-meaning.
3. A prospective client is simply an individual you have identified as someone with whom you would like to consider engaging in a freelancer–client relationship.
4. You may already have an idea of where this is headed.
5. If you only pick up one thing from this book, it's that I hope you have or can find people who can put your circumstances into perspective when you're doubting yourself or are unsure of what's going on in your life. Sometimes, those individuals can be hard to find. But if you're networking—even if only online—you're going to eventually connect to the right people.
6. Or maybe it was not so unthinkable, considering the circumstances and how the world was forced to change.

CHAPTER 3

Your Network

It's More Than the Contacts You Collect—It's Your Community

The words "network" and "networking" are two words that can cause intense feelings to rise up in people. At its most negative, networking is transactional.

You give me your card. I give you mine.

I'll send you a message when I need something from you, and you do the same.

I'll only reach out to you when I'm looking for a job.

Bet our network can be and *should be* much more than that. You're not going to know everyone in your network well, but there can be people whom you've gotten to know, whom you trust, and whom you can rely on, whether or not you ask them if they know of any gig that might be good for you. You can invite them to speak with you at a conference, you can ask them for advice, or they can, you know, just be a good friend.

IN SEARCH OF COMMUNITY

While I was getting into the industry and going to my first conferences, I had a few friends and acquaintances I would see regularly who were also new or striving to get in as freelancers. Some of them went on to have success, whether that success came quickly, or it was a slower grind for them to come to a place where they felt established in their business. Some of

DOI: 10.1201/9781003199779-4

them didn't make it. I don't mean that as if they failed—freelancing didn't work out for them for different reasons. For the ones who stopped pursuing freelancing, I thought about why. The one common factor I noted with all of them was that they didn't have a support system behind them.

For whatever reason, their friends and family at home didn't support them, and they never had a chance to develop a network around them they could rely on. I can't stress how important having support from your community is while you're trying to get your bearings. Whether that support is emotional or financial, when it's missing, it can be hard for anyone trying to make it in the game industry (let alone freelance) to press on.

You might find yourself in a similar situation. Maybe you have family who don't "get" why you just can't go out and apply for a regular job or why you can't be employed in the industry. You may not know anyone around you who's in the industry or who even cares about games. There are avenues for you to connect with like-minded people. Discord servers, Facebook groups, even the conversations you can have on Twitter threads are ways you can hear voices that get what you're trying to do. You may not even know them very well, but if you post how difficult it's been to find work—or even that you're looking for work—you're going to reach a group of people who understand you and can give you that emotional boost when you need it.

If you don't know anyone in the industry, this can be the start of your networking to build up a community that gets to know you. And one of the benefits of being in an online group is you can stay as anonymous as you want or even lurk. Sometimes just reading posts can remind you that you're not the only one who is out there trying to make a go of it in games.

So, how does networking become a source that can reenergize you, as well as be a source of income?

The business section of the book will have tips on online networking, so this chapter will talk about networking face to face. At some point, in-person networking *will* become the norm again.

THE ART OF NETWORKING

"Hi! My name is Toiya Kristen Finley. I'm a writer and editor in general. In games, I'm a game designer, narrative designer, game writer, editor, and consultant. I'm also on the executive board of the IGDA Game Writing Special Interest Group.

"What do you do?"

And that's how many conversations at networking events begin.

Do you dread walking up to a complete stranger and giving them the abbreviated bullet points of your résumé or CV? (Some of you might feel singled out reading this.) You might be introverted. Talking about yourself feels like you're full of yourself. Or maybe you're from a culture where you don't just walk up to complete strangers. Networking face to face takes a lot of physical and emotional energy. I have to take a moment to get myself ready before I walk into a networking meetup or party.

What we think of typical networking is unnatural, even for those who are really good at it. We collect 200 cards and never talk to 198 of those people we meet again. But what we consider the typical art of networking should only be part of it. Networking should be more personally and professionally fulfilling than hopping from event to event, collecting business cards, adding people on LinkedIn, and hoping we meet the right person who can help us.

While I will discuss what we think of as traditional networking and why it's so important to freelancers, I also want to give you a new way of thinking about and approaching networking as a way to build your own community.

THE NETWORK AS A COMMUNITY

My favorite state of being is in my room alone with maybe one or two dogs, but I've come to enjoy networking. I thought about why that is. I realized that I don't just have professional networks—I'm a part of networking *communities.*

I became a part of two communities in my first two GDCs 13 and 12 years ago: The Black game dev community, and the narrative community. Much of how I view networking communities is due to them.

A few years ago, a member of my Black dev networking community suggested a peer give me a call. His friend was in the same program and was about to graduate. He was going to attend his first GDC. Since this student was older and looking to get into game writing, our mutual friend thought it would be good for him to talk to me and find out what he could expect at the conference.

I suggested he go to parties to network.

"Oh, I don't want to go to any parties."

That was a shock. I asked him why he didn't want to go. "I don't like to drink that much, and they're going to expect me to drink."

This blew my mind. This was so outside of my experience that it was like listening to someone living in an alternate dimension. Finding and going to parties was the thing *everybody* wanted to do.

I said, "I don't drink. No one's ever made a big deal about it. Who said you have to drink?"

"The students here. They say you have to drink, and buy other people drinks. Nobody will take you seriously if you don't."

It would take a while to untangle the effed-upedness of executives allowing students to buy them drinks, especially knowing those students are doing it because they're desperate to get jobs, but I shared that my experiences networking at parties had been different.

SOME CHARACTERISTICS OF CULTURE

What we had in that conversation was a culture clash.

A major reason why I didn't realize there was pressure to drink in some industry circles was because I was a part of two networking communities where that wasn't emphasized. I have friends who drink. I have friends who don't drink for a variety of reasons. I personally think that if robots had bile, it would taste like alcohol, but nobody's ever pressed me about drinking.

Every community has a culture shared between its members. While I learned drinking (or not) was no big deal, he learned that it was. Communities share values, and behaviors, and ideals. The communities I was a member of made sure everyone who was in the group felt like they were a part of it, that they were welcome. The student community he was a part of, which was a networking community in its own right, made him feel singled out and different.

At one of my first GDCs, I went to a narrative meetup at a pricey restaurant. I bought about $12 worth of appetizers. But because we had to split the check, I ended up spending about $35. That was a good chunk of my food budget for the week. I was pretty vocal about that, and now we're more aware that, "Hey, we've got to find spaces where no one's going to have to spend a lot of money." There might be students in the group or devs who don't have the best financial circumstances at the moment. So, we've changed, too.

SOME CHARACTERISTICS OF COMMUNITY

Here are some characteristics of community, which apply to our networking communities. Instead of trying to collect as many pokébusiness cards as we can, our in-person networking experiences will be more fulfilling if we put the focus on relationships. We have shared values and goals, which means we're going to care about each other's personal and professional growth. We're going to want everyone to sense that they belong, and to know they're emotionally and physically safe.

BUILDING SUPPORTIVE NETWORKING COMMUNITIES

We can be a part of multiple networking communities, whether they're large or small. Whether they're focused around a particular discipline or practice, whether they're made up of specific marginalized communities, or whether they're a small group of friends. And we want to establish for our communities a culture that's going to benefit everyone.

Always be professional. It shouldn't have to be said but, sadly, it does. You've probably been in situations where people haven't been professional, and it's made the wrong lasting impression on you. You can certainly have fun at events, but you always want your behavior to reflect well on you and anything and anyone you're representing.

Seek out like-minded people, and maintain relationships. Have you ever been to an event where you didn't know anyone, and you wondered if you'd meet somebody who was like you or interested in the things you found important? You're probably going to run into someone with those same concerns, especially at large conferences. Make them feel welcome. Let them know about meetups, talks, or groups that might interest them and make their experiences more worthwhile.

This is more than paying it forward. I've found that I want to maintain relationships with some of the people I meet. I'm not saying talk to them every week or month. That's going to be impossible for a lot of us. But some of my friends I only see once or twice a year at conferences, and it's great to catch up with them.

Model the community's cultures and values. We can teach networking and relationship building just in the way we interact with others. I knew *nothing* about networking 13 years ago. I learned a lot by watching my Black dev friends. If you ask someone, "Hey, what do you want to get out of the conference this year?" Or when you talk to them about sessions or parties they might be interested in, they'll see that they can have those same types of conversations with others.

An important part of a community is member safety. People need to know they can be themselves. We can model acceptance of others. As far as drinking goes, if we don't ask, "Why don't you drink?," it doesn't become a big deal. A kind gesture I've experienced is someone buying a round of drinks for everyone. If you have the financial means and that's something you'd like to do, be mindful of people's drinking preferences. Show that it's okay for people to drink whatever they want—with no explanations.

Be mindful of members' needs and aspirations. A need can be something greater that helps someone realize their goals, or it can be small, day-to-day things. For example, if someone in your group is a vegetarian or has other dietary restrictions, make sure you go to restaurants where they can actually eat. Yeah, that doesn't seem like something that has to be said, but it does. When the Game Writing SIG plans meetups, we look at restaurants with good vegetarian options. As I mentioned earlier, I got stuck with a pricey bill, and I wasn't the only one. Several major conferences are in cities with a high cost of living. Keep in mind who'll be coming to your dinners and lunches. They might be on tight budgets, especially if they're students, freelancers, and devs who are looking for work.

When my friends and I ask each other what we're looking to achieve at a conference, we're going to get chances to help each other out. An answer to "What are you looking to get out of this GDC?" might be "Well, I really need a Maya expert." If I'm at a party and happen to meet a Maya expert, I can make the introduction.

If you're part of a marginalized or disenfranchised group, sharing this kind of information with your supportive networking community will get you seen and heard. And you're going to have opportunities through referrals by letting other members of your networking community know what you're wanting to do. Sometimes, it's difficult to talk about what we need and the struggles we might be having, but it can be a little easier to bear fruit when we share with our network. That's what happened when our mutual friend got me in touch with the student who didn't want to drink. He was able to share something that he thought put him at a disadvantage, and I was able to connect him to people who were more interested in his talent.

Introduce awesome people who should know each other! I've met a lot of awesome people over the 13 years I've been working in the industry, and sometimes I'm surprised when these awesome people don't know each other. I like to introduce people, especially when I know they have common goals and interests. It also helps to build new relationships within my own network.

Identify and promote safe spaces. There are parties and meetups that are for women, and devs of color, and the LGBTQIA+ community. A lot of people don't know about them, especially when they're new to a conference or the industry. I was introduced to the Black game dev community at my first GDC, and men whom I now consider good friends went out of their way to make sure I knew about a party thrown every year there. Now, when I see a new face, one of the first things I do is tell them about that party.

Go together! You accomplish a lot if you attend events with a friend or small group of friends. For some of you, you may have had terrible experiences trying to network, whether you were physically or emotionally threatened. Your friends can have your back in these situations. Or you might offer protection. You're a physical force to be reckoned with, or you have the type of personality that can put someone in check.

There are other reasons to go with members of your community beyond safety concerns. You might decide that you're going to go to five parties. But you're kind of talkative, so your friends can be there to step in and end conversations. Plus, you get to hang out with your friends. That's always a good reason. It's even better when you don't see those friends often.

Call out unacceptable behavior. I have "Call out unacceptable behavior" after "Go together" because I realize that calling out behavior can sometimes put us into dangerous situations. It's easier to deal with people in these situations when we're not alone.

There are different degrees of unacceptable. Someone may not realize they're using ableist language, and that's easy to explain. However, there are times when we need to cut people loose. I try to get along with everybody, and sometimes we want everything to be puppies, kittens, cupcakes, and rainbows. However, an important thing to remember about communities is that they do *exclude* people. People will prove to you that they don't deserve puppies, kittens, cupcakes, and rainbows. I mentored a student one year at GDC, and as I was packing to get on my flight in the morning, he started texting me…Propositioning me. Now, I don't know if that was his way of saying thanks, but booty call requests are not the best way to show your gratitude. I told him to go home to his wife and kids. One of my friends had invited that student to work on a project. After I told him what happened, I never saw or heard from that student again, and he certainly hasn't been around any of my circles. If they're toxic, shoot 'em out the airlock, and be done with them.

But you *are* going to meet awesome people, and 13 years from now, those relationships will still be important to you. So, a nonalcoholic cheers to everyone reading! And here's to building your networking communities!

EXERCISE

Are you currently a part of any online freelancing or game development communities? Are you a part of any online communities dedicated to your discipline?

If the answer to either question is no:

1. Conduct a search for communities that are relevant to your interests and goals.

2. Get a feel for the communities' cultures and the individuals involved. (This can be difficult with some online groups, as you have to join before you can access any content.)

3. Join the community, if you're comfortable in doing so.

CHAPTER 4

Be Kind to Yourself

YES, THERE'S A HEART in the title of this chapter. Is it corny? Yeah, probably. But I hope it's a visual reminder for the advice herein. If you're getting down on yourself, and all of a sudden a silly, red heart emoji pops up in your mind? I will have done my job.

The freelance life for many is a solitary one. Even if you're a part of a co-op or partnership, you may not work in the same physical space as your partners. I call myself a lone wolf or an outdoor cat who sometimes plays nicely with indoor cats for a reason. You may have family members and friends who have no idea what your work life is like, what it's like to be a freelancer, or your mentality as a freelancer. You may work alone, with no one else around, and you don't have opportunities to find a sounding board or sympathetic ear when you need to vent or talk through a problem. Even when you're working with partners, you can have bad moments or days. It's good to course correct and get things back in perspective. Hopefully, these tips will help you do that.

KNOW THAT YOU'LL MAKE MISTAKES

Nobody plans to make mistakes, but you're going to make them. The mistakes can range from embarrassing to upsetting, but they're going to happen.

There are going to be times when you realize you could have asked for more money—maybe a lot more money.

There are going to be times when you take on a job that's a lot more work than you expected.

DOI: 10.1201/9781003199779-5

I've made both of these mistakes and, yes, I kicked myself over them. The best way for me to get over mistakes is to learn from them what I could. As far as how much I was making and how much I *could* make, I had to realize that prospective clients and the industry as a whole had a different view of my experience than I did. I'm still learning when it's a good time to reassess my rates.

EXPECT IMPOSTOR SYNDROME TO POP UP

Here's one of the most comforting things I've ever heard in the game industry: a veteran of over 40 years told me he still got nervous before he took the stage at a conference.

Someone that respected who was used to giving speeches still got nervous and worried how he would be received? I was floored. The specter of impostor syndrome might hover about, waiting at any moment to ask, "Ya miss me?"

The key is to mitigate the hold it may have over us. Opportunities may come that we may not think we're skilled enough for, but we would be great for the project. Years ago, a friend recommended I apply for a position at a AAA studio. There was *no way* I could work at a major studio. All of my projects had been indie titles, and most of my clients had come from Elance. But while I didn't know I could do the job, others did. Did I get that job? No. But I went pretty far in the process, despite working on those smaller games. How did I get the courage to apply? While I was still mulling over all of the reasons I wasn't qualified, I also listened to the voices that said I was. Not getting the job was not a validation of my impostor syndrome. Applying at all was a huge win for me.

Overcoming moments of impostor syndrome means we're going to have to do things that make us uncomfortable. We have to learn what's possible in order to overrule what we believe is impossible.

YOU'LL PROBABLY LEARN SOMETHING NEW ON EVERY PROJECT

Something I hear my friends say is that they learn something new, or they take away a new perspective on every game they've worked on. I've found this to be my experience, too. This could mean that you learn how to use a new program or scripting language or pick up a new skill. If you're working with tech you're not used to, it might take you a while to get comfortable with it. Give yourself the grace to know that you may not get it right the first few times, and don't be embarrassed if you have to ask for help troubleshooting a problem. Asking for help is certainly better than the alternative. (And your team will be much more appreciative of you if you reach out for help instead of letting something remain broken.)

Working with a new program or time management app can also be intimidating. Know that your team wouldn't give you access if they didn't believe you were capable. Everyone new to a team is going to have to get used to the team's favored programs and ways of doing things.

But what you learn can also make you better at what you do. It may not be learning a new service or platform. It may be learning how to communicate better or adding a problem-solving tactic to your arsenal.

A new project may mean you'll be using technology you've never used before or might not be comfortable with. You might be communicating in ways you're not used to, or using processes and workflows that are new to you. Take all of this as an opportunity to refine your skills and use what you've learned on this project in your future work.

NOT GETTING A JOB DOESN'T MEAN YOU'RE BAD AT WHAT YOU DO

The sad truth is that if you're working in games and constantly looking for work, your applications will get rejected. A lot. You'll get sick of hearing "no" and, most of the time, you won't even know why.

Rejection is something that's baked in. Everybody's been rejected, more times than they'll want to admit.

I hate to say, "Get used to being rejected," but you need to. You could be one of hundreds of freelancers vying for one gig. Keep looking for more opportunities while you're waiting. Rejection may sting for a while, and you may never quite get over it, but you get to a place where you can shrug it off. The way you learn that lesson? Get rejected. Over and over and over and over. Know that unless you're told why you didn't get the job, there are any number of reasons why you weren't selected. Not getting the job doesn't mean you're bad or unskilled—it just means you didn't get that particular opportunity.

TAKE CARE OF YOUR HEALTH

I sometimes hear the perks my friends have at their studios, and I wish I could have a few of those, too. Some developers make sure that their employees take breaks and have access to different stress relievers like old school arcade consoles, coffee and tea bars, and meditation rooms. While the arcade consoles might be pricy, and we might not be able to build a whole new room onto our houses or apartments dedicated to relaxation, we do have some life hacks available to us.

Freelancers working from home don't have anyone telling them when they need to take breaks or to get up and stretch. These are things we need to do for ourselves.

Taking Care of Your Physical Health

Yeah, this is obvious, but how many of us violate this very foundational part of our lives? It's really easy to fall into bad habits without reminders, like making sure we're sitting properly and getting enough water.

Get enough sleep. Your schedule might fluctuate because of your projects and your teams' time zones, but you *can* set your own schedule. How much sleep one needs differs from person to person, but you probably have an idea of how much is enough. You should set time for quality sleep into your schedule.

Take naps! (Not required, but I highly recommend them!) Remember when we were forced to take naps as kids? Remember how we hated that? Know how you wish you could take naps during the day as an adult? You're a freelancer! There's nobody to tell you you can't.

Get a comfortable, ergonomic chair. If you don't take my word on anything else, please believe me on this one! I sat in a hand-me-down, broken-down chair for years because I couldn't afford a decent one. And I made an excuse to myself that there would be the issue of finding time to put together a new chair. That would *at least* take me five hours. My neck and shoulders suffered for years because I waited so long to get a new chair. I spent as much time shifting to get comfortable as I did writing. Eventually, I was at a convention and decided to splurge on a chair on a whim—and because I was tired of sore shoulders and a sore neck.

Protect your eyes. Chances are that if you're telecommuting from home, you're spending a lot of that time in front of a desktop or laptop (and maybe even more than one monitor). Digital eye strain is a real concern. Just like it sounds, our eyes can get strained from using computers and digital devices like smartphones, tablets, e-readers, and handheld consoles. Strained eyes "may feel tired or uncomfortable…You may not be able to focus normally."[1] I can tell when I've been in front of my laptop too long. My eyes feel tired, even though I'm wide awake, and the rest of my body feels fine. My exhausted eyes make *me* exhausted.

When we're too close to our screens, are exposed to screen glare, have bad posture while we're using our digital devices, and/or already have vision problems, we can suffer digital eye strain.[2]

What are the symptoms of digital eye strain?

Digital eye strain can cause many symptoms, including:

- Blurred vision

- Double vision

- Dry eye

- Eye discomfort

- Eye fatigue

- Eye itching

- Eye redness

- Eye tearing

- Headaches

- Neck and shoulder pain

Most of these symptoms are short-term (temporary). They often lessen or go away when you stop using your computer or device. But symptoms may continue for a longer time.

Advice from Cedars-Sinai's website. For more on digital eye strain, what causes it, and how to avoid it, visit https://www.cedars-sinai.org/health-library/diseases-and-conditions/c/computer-vision-syndrome.html.

There are a few practical things you can do to avoid digital eye strain.

- **Step away from your computer.** Physically get up from your computer and walk away. Sitting for long periods of time isn't healthy, anyway. Getting up and walking around for ten minutes also helps prevent blood clots.[3] If you have a disability that makes it difficult to get up and walk around, incorporate some stretches into your routine that can get your blood circulating.

- **Make sure to blink or use lubricating drops.** Blinking periodically and drops will help protect your eyes from dryness.[4]

- **Adjust the screen to minimize glare.** Move your screen to an angle where it's not reflecting harsh light. [5]

Drink water. Stay hydrated. Have water near your workspace that you sip on throughout your workday. And when you get to the bottom of the bottle or cup, it's a good excuse to get up from your computer and walk around to get more water. There are a number of reasons why we need to drink enough water each day. One you might not be aware of: when you don't get enough water, it "impair[s] cognitive function and decrease[s] physical performance."[6] Dehydration can make you tired, too.

These are just some methods for staying healthy while you're working at home. You can find a lot more that meet your lifestyle needs through a little research.

Taking Care of Your Mental Health

We're becoming more and more aware about the importance of self-care. As freelancers, we need to extend that to our work life and the way we think and feel about what we do.

Change your environment. If you have a space you always work in, consider leaving that space for an hour or two and finding someplace else to work. This recharges your brain and helps you rethink what you're working on. Once a week, I leave my regular space and spend the whole day somewhere else. I find I get a lot done when I do this, especially when I'm blocked on something. Part of the reason for this, I think, is that I have dedicated a special time during the week to get refocused. I don't want that time to go to waste.

Enforce breaks. Whether you have to schedule them into your calendar daily, or you take them at random, find the time to *stop*. Grinding away and feeling that you *have to* grind away is so easy to do. Force yourself to take some breaks and relax for a bit.

Find time for things you enjoy. A cliché with freelancers is that "Hustle never dies." We live through the cycle of look for a new opportunity/make your own opportunity → work on the project (while looking for the next opportunity) → finish the project → repeat. We're always networking, always searching, always trying to make new connections or reconnect *while* we're working gigs. That cycle becomes stressful, especially when you're not finding work.

This attitude can hurt us, though, if we're not finding other means of fulfillment. Life can't be a constant hustle. This can be a difficult mindset to get out of, especially when you currently don't have work, and you're under financial pressures. However, there *is* downtime. There will come times when you've exhausted all of your current leads. You will have periods where you're waiting for someone to get back to you, and you can't work *every* hour of the day.

Maybe you can't find time for it every day, but do find space to do things you enjoy that aren't related to your freelance business. Pursue your creative outlets. Catch up with friends. Go out for a walk or a jog. Pursue your hobbies—or find a new one! Recharge your body and your mind.

DON'T COMPARE YOUR LEVEL OF SUCCESS TO ANYONE ELSE'S

Yeah, this one is *hard*. You see how well your friends are doing, and while you're happy for them, you're a bit (or, you know, a lot) jealous of them at the same time. This can lead you down a bad spiral because you wonder why you're not as successful. Where are they getting their opportunities? How are they getting discovered when you're not?

There was a period when I would introduce my friends to a prospective client or employer, and they got the job, while I was still looking for something—*anything*. I can't stress how personal everyone's business is. This includes the opportunities you get and when you get them. My friends were looking for employed work, or they were artists or programmers who weren't looking for writing jobs like I was. Just because your friends are doing well, this doesn't mean you're not talented. It doesn't mean you'll never find work. Freelancing has its ebbs and flows, especially when you're trying to get established. Comparing what's happening in your business to someone else's isn't going to serve you, and it will erode your confidence.

Having said all of that, I know it's hard not to. There are so many places online and in your networking circles where you can be reminded of your down periods. If you catch yourself making comparisons, give yourself the gentle reminder that you and your businesses are different, and keep fighting to get your own opportunities.

REACH OUT TO YOUR FRIENDS

It's important to have friends who understand what you do, are freelancers or have been freelancers themselves, and work in this difficult industry. The longer you're in the industry and the more you get to know people, you'll intuitively know whom you can reach out to when you're feeling down or needing a sanity check.

Maybe you're in a difficult work situation. It's frustrating, you want some perspective, and you want some advice on how to navigate the personalities involved. Maybe you're burnt out and need someone empathetic to listen. Maybe you're just exhausted and need a break to send some goofy memes or talk about the last thing you watched.

Sometimes, you need human contact to know you're not alone, isolated at your computer. It's okay to say that you're not okay or that you're having difficulty with whatever it may happen to be—this isn't a sign of weakness, and it doesn't mean you're failing in your freelancing business.

Keep in mind the friends you can send a quick message to over social media or e-mail, or whom you can plan a quick video chat with at the spur of the moment. Even if they're busy themselves and don't have a lot of time to talk, you know you'll get a message from them.

Just don't vent in public!

BECAUSE THIS ISN'T EASY…

I can't stress enough how hard it is to be in the process of making games, let alone *finishing* games. When we're freelancers who are responsible for finding our own work, establishing our own schedules, and finding the best environments for us to be productive, we need to gently remind ourselves to keep what the freelance life entails in perspective and do the little things that can aid us mentally and physically.

EXERCISES

Chair Check

What's the state of your office chair? Is it a good fit for your body? Do some research on ergonomic chairs, and see if it's time for you to make a change.

If you need to buy a new chair, look for the best deal on the style you want.

Some stores will assemble the chair for you for a fee. Otherwise, schedule time to assemble your chair. This can take a good chunk out of your day or evening.

Break Time!

Plan breaks for your work day. Add these to your calendar. If you don't want to use a calendar, be mindful of when you're going to take your breaks, like on every half hour, after you finish sending a certain batch of messages, etc.

Also think about what you're going to do during your breaks. Will you get up and do some stretches? Refill your water? Go for a walk if you can? Meditate?

NOTES

1. "Computer Vision Syndrome," Cedars-Sinai, accessed November 9, 2021, https://www.cedars-sinai.org/health-library/diseases-and-conditions/c/computer-vision-syndrome.html.
2. "Computer Vision Syndrome," Cedars-Sinai, accessed November 9, 2021, https://www.cedars-sinai.org/health-library/diseases-and-conditions/c/computer-vision-syndrome.html.
3. Neha Viyas, "6 Tips for Taking Care of Yourself While Working from Home," last modified September 2, 2020, https://health.usnews.com/health-care/for-better/articles/6-tips-for-taking-care-of-yourself-while-working-from-home.
4. Neha Viyas, "6 Tips for Taking Care of Yourself While Working from Home," last modified September 2, 2020, https://health.usnews.com/health-care/for-better/articles/6-tips-for-taking-care-of-yourself-while-working-from-home.
5. "Safeguarding Your Sight," Harvard Health Publishing, accessed November 9, 2021, https://www.health.harvard.edu/healthbeat/safeguarding-your-sight.
6. "The Important Habit You're Missing While Working from Home," Health & Performance Collective, last modified July 15, 2020, https://healthandperformancecollective.com/why-you-need-to-keep-hydrated-when-wfh/.

CHAPTER 5

What a Freelancer Is, and What a Freelancer Is Not

A CURIOUS THING SOMETIMES HAPPENS when I've given talks about freelancing. In the reviews, I'll get angry comments from freelancers that they don't need to hear what a freelancer is. I *always* define what a freelancer is when I'm giving a talk or leading a roundtable where people new to freelancing or those interested in freelancing might be present.

The thing is though—why the anger? Why do people get annoyed that I bring it up, and they want me to know that they're hostile to it? Here's the sad thing I've discovered. There *are* veteran freelancers who don't know their power as someone who has their own business. They think of themselves as employees, and their clients as employers. I'm not being nitpicky. How you think about yourself and the language you use about yourself will shape how you see yourself, affecting how others see you, too. If you act like an employee with a client, they'll become more and more likely to treat you like one. Clients who look to scam freelancers or who are simply misinformed about freelancing tend to think of freelancers as employees, and freelancers need to learn how to identify these prospective clients and avoid them. So, to anyone who might be offended, I'm not talking down to you. But I am going to keep defining what a freelancer is because

DOI: 10.1201/9781003199779-6

freelancers can end up in awful situations when they don't understand who they are.

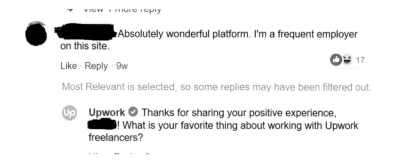

A client who views freelancers as employees.

Remember that the very nature of the freelancer is baked into the etymology of the word. You are a "free lance" who determines whom you will work with. The original meaning of the word is a mercenary. Does that sound kind of cutthroat? Yep. It's *literally* there in the word's meaning.

Freelancing is a business. You are self-employed as a freelancer, which means you're your own boss. You determine your work hours, and you are responsible for your work schedule. You decide on what days you're going to work. You determine whom you do and don't want to work with. You can terminate a contract or fire your clients. You establish what your work is worth and how much you will be paid. You determine on which projects you will and won't work. You decide how many projects you will take on at any given time.

To sum it up, a freelancer

- is one's own boss (self-employed),

- chooses whom to work with,

- has the power to fire clients,

- establishes the value of one's work,

- determines one's work schedule, and

- chooses projects to work on.

Because you are a freelancer, you are not eligible for employee benefits. For example, in the United States, you will not be eligible for worker's compensation, nor will you get health care coverage unless you pay for your own plan.

You are not an employee—you are in a collaborative relationship with your clients. They are not your bosses. There are freelancers with years of experience who have the employee mindset. You want to avoid this because *you* want to be in charge of your business, not your client.

All right. Back to your regularly scheduled reading experience.

CHAPTER 6

The Telecommuting Freelancer Starter Pack

THE SECOND PART OF this book focuses specifically on freelancing as a business. Before we get into that, there are a few basics you'll need to get started. If you've been freelancing for a bit, this will probably be a review for you.

A HOTSPOT

No telecommuting freelancer should be without a hotspot! Tethering using your mobile phone may not be enough sometimes. I've had my Wi-Fi go down and been in places where I couldn't get my laptop to connect to a network. (Strangely enough, while working on this chapter, I was writing at a location where I could usually connect to the Wi-Fi network. On this particular day, it was impossible!) I actually bought my first hotspot during GDC one year because my laptop couldn't connect to the hotel network. You may find yourself in similar, frustrating circumstances. A hotspot gives you your own dedicated access to Wi-Fi and keeps you from losing valuable time.

Depending on where you are, these probably won't be too expensive, especially since your hotspot won't be your primary access to the Internet. You'll need to buy a hotspot device and a data plan.

DOI: 10.1201/9781003199779-7

PORTFOLIO SAMPLES

Your portfolio is the evidence that you can do what you say you can. For writers, the portfolio shows the types of games you've worked on/can work on, your familiarity with genre settings, your strengths writing for particular tones and styles, and your overall range as a writer.

Whether your portfolio is public or private, you've got to have some samples ready when you start searching for work. One of the first things a prospective client will want to see are samples of what you can do, especially samples that fit with their type of game.

Portfolios get their own chapter (Chapter 10, "The Online (?) Portfolio"). We'll cover what you should include and why there.

BUSINESS CARDS

Even if you don't have a business set up, you still need business cards with as much contact information as you feel comfortable sharing. Mention what you do (programmer, composer, animator, etc.), add a special niche if you have one, and/or include a memorable slogan. You might even make space on one side of the card for people to jot down notes, by printing "Notes" or "What We Talked About" and plenty of white space to write.

A SHARPIE

A Sharpie is a must when you're networking. It can write on almost any surface, including glossy cards. If you don't like thicker pen tips because they're more difficult to write with, Sharpies do come in all tip sizes.

Why do you need a Sharpie? You might want to write on your card what you talked to someone about before you hand it to them, so they'll remember you better. When they give you their card, you can write notes on it to help you remember them and your conversation. Or, if they've run out of cards, you can give the Sharpie to them, to get them to write down their contact info for you. Don't let them tell you, "I've got your card. I'll get in touch with you." You most likely will never hear from them again.

You might also run out of cards, so you'll need something to write down your information.

N.B. In some cultures, especially in East Asia, writing on a business card is a huge no-no. The card represents one's company, and writing on it is like defacing it. If you want to write notes on someone's card, *don't—* absolutely *do not*—do it in front of the person.

INVOICE TEMPLATE

Have a good invoice template that you can use on any job. You might need several, one for each type of payment structure you use (hourly, weekly, etc.). You want to have an invoice template handy, so you don't have to format an invoice doc for every job you have. With a template, all you need to do is plug in your numbers for each project.

Information You Need on Your Template

Templates can get pretty detailed, or they can be simple. Information most commonly found on invoices are:

- The invoice number. (When you do more than one job for the client, you can have invoices numbered as 01, 02, 03, etc. Additionally, you would have multiple invoices for a client if you're being paid hourly, weekly, etc., and you turn in your invoices every two weeks, every month, etc.)

- Date you're sending in the invoice.

- Your name, business name (if you have a business name), and contact information.

- Your client's contact information. If you're not sending it to someone in particular at a company, you can remove the company-specific field and just send it to the client directly.

- Your rate for the project.

- Total time worked (hours per day, total number of hours, etc.).

- A description of the type of work done. For example, this could be "Up-front payment," "Researching audience," "Meeting with artists," etc.

- Where to send the payment. This can be your PayPal e-mail address, your checking or savings account information for a direct deposit, or other ways to send your payment.

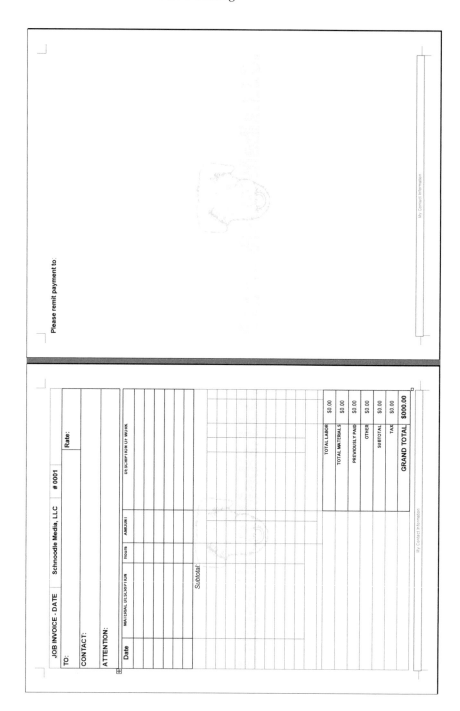

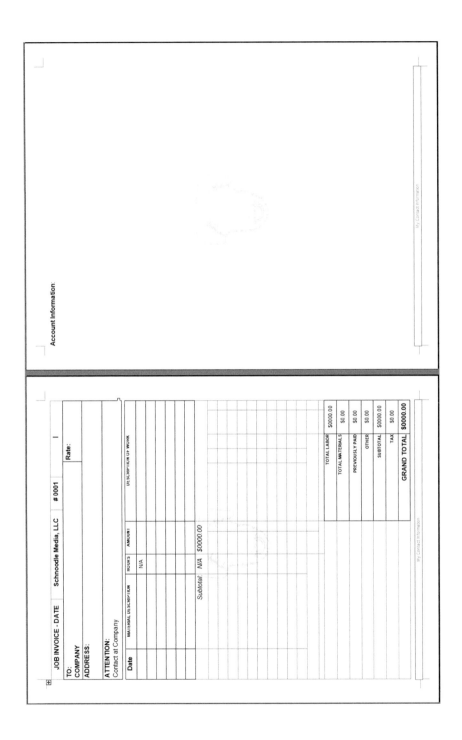

My templates are as basic as it gets. I found these templates online years ago and edit them to fit each of my projects.

Individual clients may need you to add more specifics, like a purchase order number or a contractor ID. Discuss this with the client to make sure you have all the information they need. If anything's missing, it could delay your payment.

THE KNOWLEDGE OF WHAT "WORK" ENTAILS ON A GIG

This isn't tangible like cards or a portfolio, but it's one of the most crucial things you have to understand as a freelancer. Otherwise, you could be doing work and not getting paid for it. These are tasks you'll likely be doing no matter the project, your role on the team, or payment structure.

Pre-Planning, Planning, and Preparation

Depending on how you work, you might do some pre-planning or preparation to get yourself ready for a new job. This could be anything like setting up your workspace, making a work calendar, setting up space on cloud storage, and onboarding with the team to get you comfortable with the project and the technology you'll be using.

Brainstorming or Free Association

Brainstorming or free association might be such a natural part of your process that it doesn't feel like work. Whether you write out notes, sketch, or visualize, if you're doing it for a client's game, it's work.

Sometimes, you can't shut your brain off, especially when your imagination is engaged, and you're not on working hours. If you work strictly hourly or with a day rate based on a certain number of hours per day, you might consider a flat rate that takes into account any brainstorming/free association or preparations you need to make at the beginning of a gig. On jobs where I take a flat rate, I have an "initial planning" or up-front payment milestone for brainstorming and working closely with the client to lock down with the client what the story and world of the game are going to be.

Research

Research constitutes a multitude of tasks and assignments. The word "research" tends to conjure up "read up on Ancient Mesopotamian culture."

But research is so much more than studying history for worldbuilding or even analyzing statistics to understand a particular target demographic. How and what your research can be as unique as your project.

Artist References

These can be references for artists or maybe even audio references for sound designers and composers. Either you're looking for references for someone else or yourself (if you're the artist or sound designer). It can take time to find the right references, instead of something that doesn't quite illustrate your vision. Always count this as work!

Watching TV, Films, and Other Games

If you're working with an established intellectual property (IP), you need to be familiar with its world, characters, and tone. That means you need to watch shows or films based on that IP, play other games in the franchise, or watch clips of them. I've worked on several projects with well-known IP, and spent hours watching episodes and films. Engaging with the IP gets you familiar with it. Even if you're already familiar with the IP, watching shows/films or playing games gets you reimmersed in the world and helps you pick up details that you may have forgotten or missed. Believe me—fans of the IP will know if you've gotten something wrong or if it doesn't *feel* like the story and characters they love.

You may not be working with an established IP, but your client may use certain films, TV series, or games as references for what they're wanting in their own projects.

Reading Comics, Novels, and Tabletop RPG Rulesets

Similar to watching or playing media of the IP, the IP may be an existing comic or comic series, novel or novel series, or tabletop game or franchise.

Analyzing Aspects of Other Games/Media

You may need to research, watch, and/or play other games and media for a number of reasons. Maybe you need to better understand the audience that likes urban fantasy. In order to do that, you would need to read and watch some urban fantasy to understand its tropes and why they're appealing. On a job where I was the narrative designer, I researched bestseller lists for young adult novels and manga series to figure story scenarios to pitch to my client. Research is *always* a part of a freelancer's life, and you never know what form it will take!

Factor researching into every project, and take into account how much time and effort will be necessary for that research.

Attending Meetings

Any and all meetings you attend, whether they're in person, on Zoom, or another platform, should count against your hours for the day/week or be included in your flat rate.

Writing E-Mails or Other Messages

You may be sending off a lot of quick, short messages throughout your day that don't take even a minute. However, there are times when you're going to have to compose detailed, thoughtful responses or write messages for team members with important information. Set time aside for these that is part of your workday or for hours that you will spend on the project.

THIS IS JUST A START…

As "starter pack" suggests, these are just some of the tangible things and knowledge you'll need to get started. The longer you freelance, the more you'll add to your tool kit.

EXERCISES

The Invoice

Do you have an invoice template?

Do you have an invoice for different types of payment structures you might use (hourly, daily, weekly, flat fee)?

If the answer is no to either of these, do a search for invoice templates, and find a couple that you like. Save your templates in a folder where you can quickly retrieve them when needed.

If the answer is yes, review your invoices to see if you need to edit them.

- Are they easy to read?

- Can you quickly find relevant information?

- Do you need to reformat or restructure them?

- Do you need to add information?

The Business Cards

Do you have business cards?

If the answer is no, plan out the information you'll need on your business cards.

- What's the name of your business, if you have one?
- What contact information do you need to include?
- What information do you need to include that explains what you do?
- What information should you *not* include? (Hint: Don't call yourself "aspiring," "novice," "amateur," or any other descriptors that would make someone nervous about paying you.)

Then do some research on graphic designers who can design your card for you.

- How do you want your card to look?
- What's on the front? What's on the back?
- What can you afford to pay a designer?

Now, get your cards printed.

- How many cards do you need to print?
- What can you afford?

PART II

The Freelance Business

CHAPTER 7

The Skills Every Freelancer Needs[1]

MECHANICAL WRITING. DEVELOPING CHARACTERS. Conveying characterization. Plotting dramatic tension. Building worlds. Integrating story into every aspect of the game.

These are some of the creative skills storytellers develop to be successful writers and narrative designers in games.

But there are other skills that are paramount to becoming successful freelancers. These freelancing skills improve how we present ourselves, how we protect our businesses and ourselves, and how we develop into the best collaborators for our clients.

FREELANCING SKILL #1: TIME MANAGEMENT
Developing That Internal Clock

Time management is exactly what it sounds like. It's a whole set of skills within itself, but I'm emphasizing that it is a necessity as a freelancing skill. It influences a lot of your day-to-day actions. Hopefully, you're spending your time wisely and in the way that makes you the most productive with as little effort exerted as possible.

Your time management affects all kinds of tasks throughout your day and how long (and effectively) you take to execute them. That includes spending time deciding how you're going to structure your day,

DOI: 10.1201/9781003199779-9

determining whether you write an invoice or research a topic for a project next, how much time you spend doomscrolling, checking your e-mail, etc.

I'm listing time management as the first skill because it will drive (or hamper) how you run your business, how you get your work done, and how quick and effective your decision-making process will be. Keep in mind that decision-making includes what you decide to do during the day, week, and month; how much time you'll spend in your inbox; when you'll spend time e-mailing a client or messaging them on Slack, etc. For example, you might do some quick calculations in your head to determine how much time you'll trawl through your inbox before you message a client.

The more you do certain tasks (and by "task" here, I mean anything that has to do with your freelance business), the more you develop an internal clock for how long that task will take. For a recent writing gig that had a specific way of formatting the script, I came to realize writing 500 words would take me half an hour to an hour, depending how good a "flow" I got into. On another recent gig for a developmental edit, I developed a pace of an hour a chapter as I became familiar with the author's style and storytelling techniques.

Your internal clock is so important! You might be halfway through a project and ask yourself how much longer it will take you to finish. Can you take on another project now that you're halfway through? Can you take on several more? Your internal clock will help you in the moment. Maybe you can sit and write comfortably for about 30 minutes. Then, your body will let you know when you need to take a break and get up from your desk or laptop. Let's say that project you're halfway through is a short document. You know you've got about three or four more hours to go. Can you finish by the end of the night, or do you need to quit for the day?

Because you'll most likely need to work more than one job at once, time management helps you figure out how work-intensive jobs are going to be and whether you can dedicate your energy to them or not. Say you have the opportunity to work on a long script, a 20-page bible, and 100 barks. All three prospective clients need you to start the jobs *right now* if you accept. Based on what your internal clock has taught you about your own time management, you might be able take on two or all three of these jobs.

Time management is also important because clients are going to want to know how long tasks will take during the query and negotiation stages. They see *you* as the expert on this. They will most likely have their own timetable for a project's completion, which may or may not be a rigid schedule. They may look to you to help them set realistic dates for deliverables.

If you're in leadership on a project and you have a team of writers or are collaborating with other devs, you'll need to set their schedules and deliverable dates and give the client an estimated date of completion.

With experience, you also learn what work should and should not entail; your clients may not always know this, and you might have to educate them. If you've been hired as a narrative designer, that does not mean you'll also be doing the lore writing—even if you have experience writing lore. Freelancers who are just starting out sometimes have a tendency to want to do *everything*—all the writing in the game, even when the writing should be divided among different writing roles. Your client may not realize there are different writing roles, but you don't have to feel like you have to do all of the writing to please them, especially if this means an unrealistic schedule for deliverables. Your time management skills will kick in and tell you what is and isn't possible.

Experience gives you confidence. When you see a job posting, and it's similar to work you've done before, you know you can do a great job on that project. Your experience will help you figure out how much a job will cost because you'll know everything that you'll need to do. You'll know how intensive it's going to be, how long it will take you, and how much energy you'll have to put into it. Can you work on four or five projects at once? Yes, if you know how much time you need to devote to each and you can reliably turn in your work when it's due.

 INTERVIEW WITH EDDY WEBB

Eddy Webb (with a "y," thank you) is a writer, design consultant, and game and narrative designer for video games and RPGs. He's worked on over 150 books and games during his career. He has created unique game universes, such as the Realms of Pugmire. He's also worked on established properties like The Walking Dead, Mr. Robot, Futurama, Firefly, Red Dwarf, the WWE, and Sherlock Holmes. He's even won a few awards over the past decade or so. In his spare time, he advocates for more inclusion of people with hearing loss. He can be found at pugsteady.com.

What led you to pursue freelancing, instead of employment?
A combination of need and interest, honestly. I had been freelancing along with employment for 13 years before I was laid off in 2014. I struggled with

finding a new full-time job after that, so I picked up more freelance work to help tide me over. I've always felt freelance work was freeing, in a way: I could choose what projects I wanted to work on and what clients I wanted to work with, for example. As time went on, I realized that I could leverage enough freelance work to make a living (if a small one), so I gave up on my job search, created an LLC, and became a full-time self-employed freelancer. I haven't looked back since!

"Time Management" is a broad term for a set of sub-skills. How would you define it?

I define it as "getting work done consistently in the time available." Since I used to work in an agile environment, I tend to prefer the word "velocity," as I think it's more accurate, but the idea's the same. In the end, it's about figuring out how much work you can accomplish with the time you have available to you.

I identify time management as a critical skill for freelancers. Why is it so important for our business and life in general?

I think it's mainly because we're our own boss. In most cases, our clients aren't looking over our shoulders and making sure we're getting the work done—instead, we'll get some deadlines, an agreement on what needs to be done, and then we're left to our own devices. It's important to our business because we *don't* have a boss prioritizing and managing our workflow, which means we must do that ourselves. And it's important to our lives because if it's not managed, the lines between "business" and "life" get damn murky. Every freelancer I know has had a time when they're working in some way every moment they're awake, and that's not healthy long term. So, time management is just as much about knowing when to *stop* work as it is about working *well*.

What are two or three of your most important takeaways from the classes you've taught on time management?

The first is that not all planning is the same. I break planning down into three groups: what I'm working on today, what I'm working on this week, and overall workload. Each of those requires a separate way of thinking about things, and all of them are fluid. If I need to get something done today, I work on that today, and I'm not thinking about what else needs to be done this week, this month, or this year. When it's time to figure out what to work on tomorrow, then I'll think about what else I need to work on this week. And when I'm planning my weekly workload, I'll think about what my long-term plans are.

That leads into the other big takeaway: Don't keep the whole plan in your head. We must prioritize and manage our own work, but once you've figured out what you need to work on today, this hour, this minute, focus on that. Write everything else down, and forget about it. It'll be there when you're done. Just focus on what's in front of you. Knowing when and where to focus your attention is key to managing your time and getting good velocity.

Since you've taught on time management, I would figure that it's important to you. What got you interested in the subject, and how have you applied it to your own work life?

A lot of it was necessity, honestly. When I was freelancing and working full time, I didn't have much time to waste. If you've got an hour a night to get work done, that hour needs to be productive. When I went full-time freelance, I had the reverse problem: I needed to find a reason to not procrastinate because it's really tempting to put off work while you play the new video game that dropped this week.

As such, the moment-to-moment time management came to me quickly, but I wasn't doing it thoughtfully. And as time went on, I realized my workday bled into my daily life in ways I didn't appreciate. I had to find a way to make sure I was giving exactly as much time as I needed to the work, and no more. Originally, I went back to an old structure: A 9-to-5 workday. I still do variations on that, but I have learned that an hour is an hour, no matter where in the day it falls, so there have been times when I've gone for, say, a haircut or a tattoo appointment during the week, and rearranged my plan to get all my work done at various times. After a few years of that flexibility, it's hard to go back to a rigid workday!

How does good time management improve communication and collaboration between freelancers and clients?

In so many ways! On the one hand, I've learned that if you value your own time, your client will, as well. It can be hard to say, "I work only weekdays," for example, but if you can prove to your client that the work will get done in the time you've limited yourself to, they'll respect your boundaries. At the end of the day, most clients just want the work done in the time frame they need it done in.

It also helps because a client *isn't* your boss. That's hard for new freelancers (including myself) to realize, but while it's great they're not over your shoulder thinking about your day-to-day workload, it also means they might forget things important to you. If you can manage your time and follow up on missed responses, proactively deliver before milestones, and keep in communication leading up to deadlines, the client will rely more on you to handle that part of the relationship. They'll trust you more, which means they'll hire you again in the future.

What advice would you give to freelancers who are new to this concept and are developing or improving their workflows, stress management, planning, internal clocks, etc.?

A lot of my advice stems from realizing two things about people: We're bad at measuring time, and worse at multitasking. If there are things you're bad at, find ways to automate them, so you don't have to be relied on to do them.

For measuring time, I tend to use the Pomodoro Method. There's a lot to read up on it if you want but, really, it boils down to getting a timer. Use your phone, your watch, or even an egg timer, but set yourself a reasonable amount of time (like 30 minutes). When the timer goes off, take a break, then do it again. That timer not only means that you'll take more breaks, which are important for health reasons, but also means that if you accidentally fall down a Wikipedia research hole or get caught up in the latest Twitter drama, something's there to remind you to get back to work—worse comes to worst, you've only lost half an hour.

For multitasking, that's where the planning comes in. The goal of planning is to document what you need to work on when, and then forget about it. Get it to where you know what to work on now, and then focus on that while your timer's running. That includes things like meetings, e-mail, and checking social media; don't feel bad about scrolling Twitter if you've set aside time to do that! Then, once your task is done, move on to the next thing. Once the day is over, plan for the next day (and that planning is the thing you're focusing on in the moment).

What advice would you give to freelancers who already have pretty good time management skills and understand their strengths and weaknesses?

Don't get stuck into a process. If something works for you, great! But don't assume it'll always work for you. This is something I constantly struggle with, but sometimes I get a new kind of work or the work is heavier or lighter than normal, and I have to take time to step back and rethink things. Trust me—taking a half hour to reassess your workload and produce a new plan will save you hours of banging your head against a wall.

On the other hand, be wary of what I call "productivity porn." Reading the latest productivity book or spending hours on a self-help forum might *feel* like productivity, but spending hours and days revisiting and revising your processes for a small benefit is still lost time. It's okay to experiment and try new things—in fact, it's good to change things up—but don't let that thirst for the latest new tip distract you from getting the work done.

Are there particular tools or apps you'd recommend that assist with time management? What features does a good time management app or tool have?

I use Trello a lot for my planning. It's a free, flexible, and easy app that allows me to focus less on features and options and more of documenting the plan, so I can get to the plan. In fact, that's a good feature for any time management tool: Make sure it does just what you need it to do, and don't let it overwhelm you with options that distract you.

I also use a pad of paper. Sometimes, when I'm planning, I get distracted by a Slack notification or an e-mail that rolled in, and I feel like I *need* to check those because it might affect my plan (spoiler: It almost never does). I also do it when I'm in a virtual meeting, so my hands stay away from my mouse, and I don't end up accidentally checking messages when I should be paying attention. When I'm finding myself not focusing, just grabbing a plain old legal pad and writing down what I need to do can be a huge help. I can always transcribe it later, but some of my colleagues just live in that pad of paper. Some even use techniques like bullet journaling to make their paper planning tools the most effective. They don't work for me, but that doesn't mean they're bad.

In the end, the best tool to use is the one that helps you focus on the work. If having a big whiteboard helps, use that. If having an app on your phone that grows a digital tree while your focus keeps you on task, let that tree grow.

Do you use any time management apps or have techniques that focus on self-care?

The best (and simplest) app is a timer because the Pomodoro Method makes sure there's some self-care. Lots of people focus on the "do something for 25 minutes" part, but they sometimes forget the "do *one* thing for 25 minutes" and "take a five-minute break" parts. As a freelancer, it can really feel like every waking moment you need to be constantly working on a dozen different things, but taking regular short breaks and focusing on one thing at a time really helps not only your work focus, but also your mental health.

As freelancers, we're all about "hustle, hustle, *hustle!*" How do time management apps assist in breaking individuals out of harmful habits?

The beneficial part of time management is that you're…well, managing your time. Without some kind of process or external app, it's really easy to feel like you're not getting anything done, and that you need to keep working. If you manage your time, it means you can also look back on it and see what you've accomplished. In terms of self-care, that means you can more easily justify taking time off—if you're not feeling well one day, you can quickly look at your planned work for the day and spread it out over the next few days. That allows you to take a day guilt-free, without ending up spending the next several days working twice as hard.

Similarly, I highly encourage all freelancers to set office hours, or at least a set number of hours you work each day and a set number of days you work each week. Yes, once in a while you'll have to meet with a client on weekends or at odd hours. Yes, sometimes a project hits crunch mode, and you need to work more than you expected. But if you don't have office hours, you will always be taking meetings and working overtime because there are no boundaries to cross. It's better to make a conscious choice to work 50 hours this week, instead of checking your time on Sunday night and realizing you've accidentally worked 70.

Think of yourself as a company asset. If you're a self-employed freelancer, you are your company. And if you work so hard you burn out or become seriously ill, there's no one left in your company to do the work—someone else will take it on (and the money that goes with it). As such, you need to treat your company's entire workforce (i.e., you) extremely well, so you can work for a long period of time. It's a cliché to say, "It's a marathon, not a sprint," but there's a grain of truth to it because marathon runners don't run as hard as they can the entire time. You shouldn't work as hard as you can at all times, either.

FREELANCING SKILL #2: MARKETING
You're a Brand, Baby!

As a freelancer running a business, you're always going to have to market yourself and make a good impression. Marketing for freelancers entails everything from naming your business to coming up with a logo for your business to designing business cards, from maintaining an online portfolio to selling yourself while networking (and networking is its own skill) to establishing yourself as an expert in what you do and how you do it.

How you talk about yourself is also marketing, even in one-on-one conversations. You're the best representative for yourself and what you do in your business.

Words of Devalue ("Aspiring," "Novice," etc.)

What you say about yourself and your business can harm or help. Even one seemingly insignificant word you use to describe yourself can devalue you in front of prospective clients. Does that sound a little too threatening or complicated? It's not. Just make sure you eliminate a few words from your vocabulary when you talk about yourself in person or in writing.

I've attended a lot of conferences in person and online over the past decade. There's a particular way that people would introduce themselves that would astound me: "Hi! I'm an aspiring game writer!" It happens at least once a conference.

There's not one person I've met who called themselves an "aspiring game writer" (or "novice narrative designer," or "recreational game designer," etc.) who was actually aspiring. The problem is that how the person labels themselves as a novice and how the industry views them is completely out of sync. Anyone who's been a part of a game jam, DM'ed for their tabletop group, written bibles, written character bios, or, you know, *is actually writing*, is not aspiring to do anything. If you're writing, you're a writer. The only thing prospective clients care about is if you can do the job.

"Novice," "aspiring," "recreational" are all bad marketing. Don't talk about yourself that way. And please, please, *please* don't use those descriptors on your business cards, résumés, or CVs. Labeling yourself this way suggests that you lack the ability to do the very jobs you're seeking. Writers who have been publishing fiction or comics or writing film and TV scripts for years see themselves as "aspiring" when looking for game work, too, even when these individuals have more storytelling knowledge and skills than people who are already in the industry and trying to find game writing or narrative design work.

Think of it this way: I'm an indie dev, and I need a game writer for some character bios. I meet a couple of writers who are interested in my gig. One has a bachelor's in English. The other has a bachelor's in creative writing. I like their samples. One says they're a game writer. The other says they're a novice writer, and they're just trying to figure everything out. Whom am I more likely to give my money to? The person who presents themselves with confidence. When you use words like "novice" or "aspiring," you're telling prospective clients that your skills need to be better, and you're not quite ready to work professionally.

There's another problem you should consider when you present yourself as a "noob." Not everyone is honorable, and there are clients who scam and take advantage of freelancers. If scam artists think you're a novice, they'll target you to manipulate you. And predatory clients find ways not to pay you, and they'll most likely be hell to work with.

Naming Your Company

Whether you have a sole proprietorship, limited company, or co-op, your business needs a name. That name needs to be memorable and tell your audience something(s) about you. Your "audience," in this case, is *anyone* who may take an interest in you and your work.

Your name is important to your brand. It represents you, your values, and your work. When you're coming up with a name, you want to make sure that it's unique, while still being true to who you are. Before you choose a name, do an Internet search to see if there are other companies with the name you want to choose. Also look and see if anyone has registered a business under the name or a similar name.

My LLC's name is Schnoodle Media. "Schnoodle" is a portmanteau of "schnauzer" and "poodle" because schnoodles are a schnauzer/poodle mix. I love dogs. I've always had dogs, and I owned a schnoodle who lived for 16 years, Ella Es Bonita ("Ella" for short). At the time she died, she was more than half my age.

When it came time for me to come up with a name for my company, it didn't take me long to settle on Schnoodle Media. "Schnoodle" is unique. It's not a word you hear often, and it's certainly not a word in company names. It pays homage to my schnoodle and my love for dogs, but it has a greater meaning beyond that.

My business's tagline is "Entertainment of Mixed Breeding." Schnoodles are a mixed breed, and I do a mix of things as a freelancer. I'm an editor and writer, working in several media. In games, I'm a game designer, narrative designer, game writer, editor, and diversity/narrative consultant. But I also work in a mix of story genres. I've written and edited realism, fantasy, horror, science fiction, slipstream, magical realism, metafiction, romance, mystery, and suspense. "Schnoodle Media" encompasses all of the things I am and all of the things I do, and it's a name you're not likely to hear anywhere else.

 INTERVIEW WITH RACHEL PRESSER

Rachel Presser is a writer, business consultant, and game and film producer from The Bronx. With a unique blend of creative and entrepreneurial aptitude, Rachel founded Sonic Toad Media in 2015 and has been in the entertainment industry for over ten years in producer, business management, and narrative designer roles. She is also opening Amphibious Concepts Productions in Los Angeles. In her free time, Rachel rants on Medium,

goes to punk shows and retrowave nights, and can be found at reptile and amphibian sanctuaries.

What led you to pursue freelancing, instead of employment?

I always wanted my own business, but thought I had to fall in line and work a normal job first…in the post-recession economy that never improved. I don't fit the mold for normal jobs, anyway. Once I lost my last salaried job in 2014, building a website and offering my own highly niche services as I wrote, made games, and did other cool projects simply made more sense to me than fighting like hell trying to get another job.

It's a mix of entrepreneurial desires and trauma that makes working a normal job too triggering.

We have something in common in that both our business names are inspired by animals. What was your thought process in choosing Sonic Toad Media & Consulting for your business?

I've always loved toads and knew I wanted to put some kind of reference to toads in my business. Since I work primarily with the games industry, I also wanted to incorporate something that would at least SOUND like it?

After all, outlandish names and quirky names referencing animals are a norm with indie game studios!

How does "Sonic Toad" reflect you as a freelancer? Does it capture your values or a particular philosophy? What does it communicate to prospective clients?

There's a stunning number of brands that call themselves "X Toads" or "The Toad," and their branding and philosophy has zero to do with amphibians. Like, I found some creative services firm called Metal Toads and I was just—buddy, WHERE'S the toads?!

There's warty toads all over my site and branding! That's the point! They're kinda in your face! I'm known as The Toad Lady for a reason.

(Well, that, and toads are just extremely cute. How do you NOT put them all over your website?!)

Toads are an extremely underestimated and overlooked animal, and if you're a TV Tropes fan, there's some Fridge Brilliance at work there: It means that I work with the underestimated, and solve problems that frequently get overlooked.

Why is branding so important for freelancers?

Branding is how you stand out from everyone else trying to do the same thing.

We're all hustlers. We're all trying to extricate ourselves from the capitalist grind. We pick something we're good at, and we market it. Simply saying "I'm good at X" doesn't cut it. What problems do you solve? Can you catch people's attention? You can be the best programmer in the world, but clients will just scroll past your website if you post a little portfolio and nothing about you or what you stand for.

What are some branding and marketing strategies that freelancers may not think are branding or marketing? How can they start to use those strategies to their advantage?

Developing a brand voice.

It's one of those things we don't really think of because it takes time, often evolves, and trying too hard with this can seem inauthentic. But developing a brand voice can become a powerful tool for keeping your audience captivated, and your clients to continually give you money (in addition to delivering top-notch results, of course!).

What is your most important marketing "don't" for freelancers?

Don't use paid marketing (the SEM side of things) unless you really know what you're doing with it and/or have cash to burn. Namely, if you have some kind of digital product to sell, like an e-course or book. But if you're not very established yet, I don't recommend Adwords, Facebook ads, etc., until you have a more well-defined target market.

When you're a company of one and you're also the product, you're throwing your cash to the wind when you're starting out. Even if you get some decent leads out of it, ads only run as long as you pay for them— unlike social media which is free and your own content, which is FOREVER.

What is your most important marketing "do" for freelancers?

Do learn how to define your target market, and even more importantly, strategize how to properly reach them.

Remember, this can evolve over time! I got a lot of my clients at live shows, but between COVID-19 and a surgery I had prior to the pandemic, I had to put this outreach method indefinitely on hold. It made me think about the types of clients I reached versus the clients I usually get, along with what I actually wanted to do for Sonic Toad's revenue streams. I leaned harder on indie games Twitter than I ever thought I would, and got a shocking amount of business from it.

 BRAINSTORMING A BUSINESS NAME CHECKLIST

Not sure where to start when coming up with your own business's name? Here are some questions to juice your creativity:

- What's important to you?
- What's unique about you?

- What kind of work do you do?
- What's unique about the way you do your work?
- Do other companies have the name you're choosing?

Your online presence is part of marketing, including your LinkedIn profile, Twitter, portfolio, or profile on freelance sites. Any chance you have to speak in person about who you are and what you do is *also* marketing. You want to make sure you always present your business as professionally as possible.

Always brand yourself as an expert, whether you have a niche or not.

Ribbons for Schnoodle Media on my GDC badge. Photos taken by the author. Collecting as many ribbons as possible and sticking them on your badge has become a favorite activity at GDC. One year, I invested in a couple of ribbons in my logo's colors and put my logo and website on them. Also notice Rachel Presser's Sonic Toad sticker and clip above my card.

FREELANCING SKILL #3: KNOWING YOUR WORTH

Who'll Know If You Don't?

This is understanding the value of your skills and the value that you, with your insight and experience, bring to a project. As is the case with marketing yourself as "aspiring," when you don't know what you're worth, you can get scammed. You can work with clients who treat you as a cheap commodity. You might realize that *you've* undervalued a project, and you're doing a lot more work than you're going to get paid for. That can make you bitter and stressed. I *way* undervalued some projects when I started out, and it made me miserable. I was not going to get paid for all of the time and energy I was putting in. But this has made me smarter. When you know what you're worth, you're going to attract the prospective clients you really want to work with. They respect what you do, and they'll respect your asking price, even if they can't always afford it. Sometimes, and this has been the case with me, a client will end up working with me even though they end up paying more than they had allotted in their budget.

Be Aware of Your Hats and Get Paid for Each One You Wear

The more hats you wear, the more valuable your skills are to a project. This is true at studios, and you can apply this to your freelancing. My understanding and work as a game designer inform my narrative design. This is a way for me to approach prospective clients.

If I'm working on the game design and narrative design, I should be paid for both.

If I'm hired for narrative design, and I end up doing game design without additional payment, this is **scope creep**.[2] It's easy to fall into scope creep, especially if you have a good rapport with a client. You may not *mind* doing the extra work, but you really should be getting paid for anything you didn't agree to in the contract.

I had a project where I was hired to establish the worldbuilding for potential transmedia projects. The client later wanted me to take on a writing project, so we negotiated the cost for it and drafted a separate contract. Writing the transmedia was not considered part of developing the worldbuilding.

That might sound obvious, but lots of freelancers take on extra tasks because they believe they've been hired to do them, or they like the client, so they do it for free, or the client guilt trips them into it for one reason or another.

Don't Wear Hats That Don't Fit

Don't try to work outside of your skill set. If the client asks you to do something and you can't, let them know. If you realize the client needs to add somebody to their team or project because there's no one currently with that skill set, let them know that, too.

FREELANCING SKILL #4: PROTECTING YOURSELF

Know your responsibilities on a project. Know your contracts. Use the information in your contract to protect yourself against scope creep and nonpayment. The "Please Learn from My Ignorance" chapter has a very special lesson I learned in this regard.

Another way to protect yourself is to negotiate your schedule to erect boundaries. When you are available to work is in your contract, which can help keep you from overextending yourself or your client from (intentionally or unintentionally) manipulating you into doing more work.

You can also fight for the credits you want on your project. Negotiate these at the contract stage. Credits are a way of marketing in their own right. They reflect what you did on a project and the different skill sets you've used. For more on the importance of credits and how they reflect upon you, see Elizabeth LaPensée's interview in Chapter 9.

FREELANCING SKILL #5: NETWORKING

All Freelancers Have to Do It

Networking has its own chapter, but I want to address it as a skill here and how to improve it, while the chapter addresses it as a support system. Networking can be a little awkward when you're at an in-person event, and you walk up to a stranger and just start talking to them like you know them. But networking is that thing we all know we have to do. Walking up to strangers and starting conversations is a part of it.

Whether you're speaking to someone in person or online through posts on Twitter, Facebook, Discord, etc., how you present yourself and the content you choose to share is what will make you memorable…or not.

Don't simply talk about games or what you enjoy about your work. Networking is akin to marketing. During networking opportunities, learn how to discuss your areas of expertise and freelancing skills in the context of the prospective client's projects or even when you're sharing with other professionals. Show them why they need you and how you might be a part of their project. This doesn't mean that you jump into a conversation and start talking about what you do and that you're available—you should make this a natural part of the conversation.

Networking is also an opportunity to address your personal philosophies about your work/role as a developer and how you collaborate with others.

In the last few years, extensive networking has moved to online spaces. Before COVID-19 forced everyone onto Zoom calls, developers looking for work learned to use the art of conversation to their advantage in Twitter threads, Discord channels, and on Facebook posts. Conversation can start for any reason or just about any topic. I've seen posters ask for advice for everything from which website to use for their online portfolios to specific textures to use in a program. Narrative designers have started threads on how to improve communication with nonnarrative members of the team, and devs from different disciplines have chimed in with their experiences and suggestions. Someone in a group I admin would always post jobs when she found them, and she became known for this, and everyone remembered her name because of it. Even something as simple as "What's your favorite adventure game?" invites people to engage with you. And it's an opportunity for networking. How you answer that question demonstrates to prospective clients how you think about games on both personal and professional levels.

The idea is that you want to be memorable (in a good, professional way!), and you want people to think of you when they have a project where you'll be a good fit, or someone asks them for referrals.

Asking for advice, giving advice, and talking about aspects of games are all smart ways to network online.

Speaking Engagements and Networking

You have other opportunities for networking that you may not have realized were, in fact, networking. Speaking engagements are huge networking opportunities that can lead to bigger things. As a speaker, you put yourself out there as an expert on the topics you choose. This is another way to become known. Over my years of speaking at game conferences, I've moderated a panel where new writers can ask questions of veterans; I've led workshops on game design, game writing, and narrative design; I've talked about freelancing; and I've introduced concepts of how developers create a "breadcrumb language" where they give hints to players. Each of these subjects established me as an expert on these topics.

In my case, networking led to speaking engagements and book projects (including this one)! The workshop I co-led bore the fruit of several books with this publisher. I've been invited to speak at and attend conferences, which has led to referrals, repeat clients, and contributions to several books. Many of my game projects have come directly from referrals through networking, and one came because of the client's awareness of one of my books. Most jobs in the industry are hidden, meaning they're never advertised, and people ask their friends and colleagues if they know anyone who would be good for specific roles.

What should you talk about? What have you wanted to share for a long time? What is no one else talking about, and at least *somebody* should be addressing it? I usually end up pursuing topics after a few years of wondering why no one else is addressing something that I've been mulling over for a while. I started doing talks on freelancing at a time when friends would come up to me at parties or bars and ask me how they could do the whole freelancing thing. I realized this was becoming a bigger question in the industry, and it needed a platform on a much larger scale. There were a lot of freelancers and devs curious about freelancing who needed a community and resources. I started analyzing what I called a revelatory breadcrumb language after I realized it was a concept nobody else had discussed. As I've said, when I've seen a need, I've filled it. This is also an aspect of marketing because what you're an expert on is part of your brand. You're telling the game industry, "This is the stuff I know." What do you want them to know about you and the knowledge you can share?

You can pitch talks to large or small conferences. Are there smaller conferences or conventions in your area? If you're not quite ready to pitch, you can give a talk to a high school or college class. Those *absolutely* count, and you'll get great experience learning to speak to an audience, communicating effectively, and designing slides.

There are more and more online conferences. If you're not comfortable speaking in person, you can do it from the comfort of your own bedroom or workspace. With some of these conferences, you send a video of your talk. You don't even have to do it live!

FREELANCING SKILL #6: ASSESSING CLIENT NEEDS

Read between the lines of what the prospective client does and does not say. Verbalize what the client cannot. Either it's something they don't understand, and they really *need* to, or it's something they haven't considered because you're the expert. For example, they want you to develop a super-detailed world for a clicker game, but you explain that players don't expect detailed worldbuilding or stories in clicker games. They'll most likely get frustrated with a story interrupting their gameplay. Instead, you explain how you can deliver story through the art and character animations.

Some of your clients may be nondevelopers. They may not even play games. They don't have the same terminology or knowledge that you do. You may have to be patient with them to help them express what they want.

FREELANCING SKILL #7: PROFESSIONALISM

Be professional in all aspects of your business and communication. If you have a break-up, keep it professional, even if they don't. You don't want a reputation of being difficult to work with.

Dishonest clients may try to blackmail you on freelance websites. They'll promise not to leave bad feedback if you agree to receive less payment or no payment at all. Don't give in to this. Report this behavior. You may have to take a hit to your ratings and reviews. But giving in teaches clients they can bully freelancers, and it will keep you from hard-earned payments. *NEVER* refund money for work you've done.

Do help clients understand what they need, and don't wear hats that don't fit. You're going to have to help developers and nondevelopers alike understand your role and responsibilities. I worked with a client who didn't know what game bibles and game design documents were. I explained why they were necessary. The client didn't have the funds to pay me to write them, so I gave him some examples, and he wrote the game bible and GDD himself. If the project needs something that you can't provide, be generous with your advice.

Remember that, ultimately, it's not your project, and you're not the one putting money into it. You can give advice. Address your concerns. You can try to steer your clients in a certain direction. If they don't agree, don't keep pushing them.

IT TAKES TIME…

Some of these freelancing skills you will have already developed. You may already be great at networking, or you are quick to assess a client's needs and solve their problems. With other skills, it may take some time. For example, it took me a while to get a full picture of what the client wanted, what they actually needed, and how to express the difference between the two. The only way we develop these skills is through our experiences, whether that's reaching out to individuals while networking, figuring out what our business philosophies are (and seeing how those change over time), or learning to make the most of our limited time.

EXERCISE
Skill Strengths and Weaknesses

Of the skills listed in this chapter, which do you think are your strengths? Why?

Which do you think are weaknesses? Why?

For the skills you feel you can improve, how might you start strengthening them?

NOTES

1. Expanded from Toiya Kristen Finley, "Freelancing in Games: Narrative Mercenaries for Hire," in *The Advanced Game Narrative Toolbox*, edited by Tobias Heussner (Boca Raton: CRC Press, 2019), 179–201.
2. In freelancing, scope creep is work outside of the parameters you negotiate with your client, and you're never paid for that extra work.

The Freelance Life Is a Research Life (Especially When It Comes to the Legal Stuff)

Don't think of this chapter as advice. Rather, consider it a checklist of VERY IMPORTANT STUFF YOU NEED TO RESEARCH ON YOUR OWN.

This is for a couple of reasons:

1. I am not a lawyer and cannot give you legal advice.[1]

2. A freelancer's business is personal to the individual freelancer. What's right for my business may not be right for yours.

And why the all caps? You don't want to have your business up and running, only to discover that you're not running it legally.

DOI: 10.1201/9781003199779-10

Freelancers, no matter their discipline, tend to focus on their work and the things they enjoy doing, instead of the very practical matters of running their business. However, if you're a freelancer, *you are* a business owner. *You are* an entrepreneur, even if you don't think of yourself that way.

There are several important subjects you will need to look into for yourself and weigh carefully, and make sure you have addressed all legal matters (or continue to address them, in the case of things like paying taxes) to run a successful freelance business.

First, what type of business should you have, if you haven't already set one up?

TYPES OF BUSINESS STRUCTURES

I'll list the business structures that make the most since for freelancers, but this will by no means be exhaustive. What business structures you can consider depends on the country you live in and the number of people who have ownership in the business.

Sole Proprietorship

(Many Countries)
Sole proprietorships are unincorporated businesses. Unincorporated businesses are entities not separated from the business owner.[2] The business owner and the business are one and the same in a sole proprietorship.

Advantages

- Sole proprietorships can claim personal tax credits.

- They do not have to pay ongoing fees, like annual reports or filing fees.[3]

- Owners of a sole proprietorship only need to file one individual tax return.[4]

Disadvantage

- Sole proprietorships don't protect business owners from lawsuits or other liabilities, as the business and business owner are one.

Limited Company (LC)

(Most Countries)

Depending on the territory, these are known as "limited" (Ltd.), "limited company" (LC), limited liability company (LLC), or limited partnership (LP) when there is more than one member. They're *limited* because the owner's or owners' assets are separate from the business entity.

Advantage

- Your personal assets remain separate from the company. If someone sues the company, they have no rights to your personal assets, should they win litigation.

Disadvantage

- Generally speaking, limited companies are subject to more taxes and fees.

The Single-Member LLC (SMLLC)

(United States)

This is a limited company that, as its name suggests, is owned by only one person.

Advantages

- The single-member LLC protects the owner against liability, as other limited companies do.

- Single-member LLCs are "disregarded entities." For tax purposes, they're treated as sole proprietorships and can be reported on the individual member's tax returns. This cuts down the costs of preparing and filing tax returns, since the SMLLC won't need its own form.[5]

Cooperative (Co-Op)

(Many Countries)

A group of individuals own a cooperative for the purpose of using its services.[6] Each co-op member (also called a "user-owner") has an equal vote in company matters and establishes the company around a common need.[7]

Advantages

- It's easy to add members should owners wish to add to their cooperative.

- All members have equal say in the business.

- Running day-to-day operations, finding work, and delegating work are easier since these are distributed among all members of the co-op.

Disadvantage

- If every member does not put in their equal share of the work, you might have to remove members.[8]

Your Business' Articles of Incorporation

You will need to file Articles of Incorporation. Included in the articles are

- the date the business was founded,

- the address and location of the business,

- the names of the owners and a list of what percentage they own, and

- the duties and responsibilities of the owners.

You'll find templates for Articles of Incorporation online. Additionally, if you use a service to help you set up your business, the service can generate this for you.

If you use a service to help you incorporate, it can also act as your registered agent. A registered agent receives legal documentation on your behalf and passes it along to you. The benefit of a registered agent is that your personal contact information, such as your home address and phone number, is not published publicly in association with your business.

TAX ID?

Once you've formed your company, you will need to register with the proper authorities for a tax ID. In the United States, sole proprietorships do not need tax IDs because they are considered the same entity as the owner. This may also be the case if you have a single-member LLC, but check with your state if the SMLLC needs a separate tax ID from your Social Security Number.

BUSINESS LICENSE AND/OR PERMIT?

Do you need one where you live? Some municipalities and states require businesses to have business licenses and/or permits if they offer certain types of services. Permits and licenses vary by industry.

 BUSINESS FORMATION CHECKLIST

- Research business structures available in your country.
- Get legal advice on what business structure is best for you.
- Consider using a service and/or registered agent to set up your business.
- Submit any forms necessary to incorporate your business.
- Apply for any permits or licenses you may need.

 BUSINESS TAXES CHECKLIST

Research what taxes and fees you or your business will be responsible for

- at the federal level, and
- at the local level.

A NOTE ON PARTNERSHIPS AND COOPERATIVES

Some freelancers prefer to partner with each other and own multimember freelancer companies. For more information on this and why it might be a good idea, please see the interview with Ian Thomas, a cofounder of Talespinners, below.

 INTERVIEW WITH IAN THOMAS

Ian is a narrative designer, writer, and games programmer who's handled interactivity and storytelling for a living for over 25 years. He's worked in interactive television, education, puppet-making, film, publishing, and the games industry, and has contributed design, writing, or code to more than 70 games, including franchises such as LittleBigPlanet, LEGO, and, Amnesia. He's written, designed, or directed action movies, children's

books about Cthulhu, interactive fiction, RPGs that feature giant rats, and critically acclaimed larps. He founded Talespinners, the writing cooperative, and is currently Narrative Director at Ubisoft Stockholm.

Note: At the time of this interview, I was subcontracting with Talespinners.

What led you to pursue freelancing, instead of employment?

There were a few factors. At the time I decided to start freelancing, I was living in Cardiff, which was a long way geographically from any major games company, and I had no plan to move—and I was trying to switch from being primarily a coder to primarily a writer. At that time, working remotely for full-time employment was very rare among large companies, and smaller indie companies rarely had full-time writing roles, so freelance seemed a better fit. I was stuck in a bit of a rut creatively, and had been approached by a couple of indie companies to ask if I could do work on the side. I very much enjoy working on multiple projects—I thought freelancing would give me that range.

You mentioned large companies weren't really working with remote freelancers at the time you wanted more work as a writer. That has changed over the past few years. Why do you think large companies are more willing to work with remote freelancers?

It's not so much remote *freelancers*, as remote workers. And the reason why is simple—COVID-19! It's drastically changed everything. Big companies that *don't* allow any measure of remote work are now seen as behind the times—if they demand 100% on site, there are plenty of other places people can now apply to instead for better work–life balance. Sure, there are often issues around location (for legal reasons/salary/tax, etc.), but COVID-19 has proved that remote work is possible, and so the world is changing.

How did you come up with the idea of starting a freelance co-op?

We went through two iterations with Talespinners.

When I was going to go freelance, I was worried about that step of going it alone. Not only the fear of stepping into the unknown, but the lack of any sort of safety net.

So, I pitched the idea to Giles Armstrong—also a freelance writer living in Cardiff—that it would be better for us to team up together to be able to pitch for work together and back each other up. For simple practical reasons—like being able to source insurance together. Or so that only one of us needed to go to a games show to look for work, instead of both of us having to pay out for it. Or when work came in, if one of us had too much work on, the other could help them out. And, quite honestly, simply for company—freelancing is a lonely life, and having someone else to talk to about what you're working on is invaluable.

We tried it, and it worked really well. That simple act of putting a name and a logo on the partnership together made a big difference when it came to pitching ourselves. For some reason, being a "company" made us seem more serious and stable to potential clients. Work was erratic initially, as it is with any freelancing start-up, but we made a much bigger impact than we would have as individuals.

Then, later on, Giles departed to go and work on a AAA project. That left me running the company on my own, and that really didn't appeal to me. Obviously, I could have hired people to take on the projects we were working on, but there's so much stress that comes on your shoulders running a company that I really wasn't interested. I had run companies in the past and already decided it wasn't for me. But, I thought: Why not stick with the original reason Giles and I had set up the company, to back each other up, and was there any reason not to widen that? So, I pitched the idea of a cooperative to a few of the freelance writers who we'd been working with and, happily for me, they could all see the advantages. So, they all stepped up and became co-owners of the company—and that decision was vindicated. There is strength, safety, and community in numbers. In so many ways, the whole was more than the sum of its parts.

These days, Talespinners rarely has to scramble looking for clients—it has built enough of a reputation that clients come to Talespinners. Which is a real vindication of the model, I think, and its initial aims to reduce stress and bring a measure of stability.

A lot of freelancers are the only member of their business. What was it like working with partners? Did you have to alter any of your work habits to make the business model work?

It was relatively straightforward. Being a co-op, any major decisions involved everyone—but outside of that, everyone worked individually. Like any other business, there was a lot of focus on communication—keeping good records about the projects under way, tracking which potential clients we'd been talking to, making sure timesheets were kept and invoices sent out regularly. But I'm a reasonably organized person anyway, so a lot of those things would have been things I would do myself as a freelancer. Probably the biggest change was simply about learning each other's strengths and figuring out a way to decide who should take on work when it came in—finding a sensible way to weigh things so that the people in the company most in need of work at any given time would pick up the bulk of the work on a new contract.

Who is responsible for nonwriting duties, like bookkeeping and keeping track of invoices, seems to be a big part of whether a co-op is going to succeed or not. How did you learn each other's strengths outside of freelancing? Was it simply getting a feel for it the longer you worked with

each other? Did anyone's duties change once you realized they were better suited for other roles?

Simple answer is me. :-D I billed the time I spent on it at a nominal rate. I had already been involved in running companies, so I had a clue how to do all of that, and since I had been the founder, I had all of the connections and permissions set up. And it was a relatively slick and easy process— Talespinners isn't complex from an admin point of view, maybe half an hour admin a week, if that. And so, no, duties didn't really change, until I took a backseat—I carefully wrote down everything that I used to do for the company (I think there was a little surprise as to quite how many things that was from the other team members) and distributed that to the others.

Do you find that a co-op has distinct advantages over individual freelancers? How do you exploit those advantages when communicating with prospective clients?

It has huge advantages. For example:

- **Feedback:** Often, working on smaller indie projects, you may be the only writer on a game. With a co-op, all of the different members of the co-op are under the same NDA,[9] so you can turn to any of them to give you help and advice on what you're working on—and they all understand story in a way that potentially the other members of the project might not. Similarly, those other members of the team can give you advice on dealing with clients, such as whether your quotes for work are pitched at the right level, or how to handle nonpaying clients, and so on. "Am I overreacting?" is the sort of thing that really stresses out an individual freelancer, and in the cooperative, other people have your back.
- **Sharing work:** When we can, we share work around the cooperative. For example, if one member writes for a client company, another member might be able to edit it. This results in both being paid, both receiving a credit, and the client company having higher-quality work.
- **Finding work:** You can band together on things like attending games shows, or printing business cards, or placing adverts, or buying a stand at an industry event. Your profile is vastly raised over that of an individual freelancer, and the fact that you are a varied group of experts and can operate at scale is very attractive to some potential clients. It means that instead of hiring one person, they get a range of skills.
- **Bargaining:** It is much easier to negotiate with clients if you are part of a stronger team, rather than a freelancer on your own. Even the simple impression of being a company rather than a lone individual means that things like chasing invoices gets better results, but also you have more collective muscle to be able to bargain for reasonable fees and sensible deadlines.

- **Scalability:** Because we are a group, we can handle larger projects, which is attractive to clients who want a simple solution to get a reasonable amount of work done quickly.
- **Economies of scale:** As a group, we can split fees for insurance, for website costs, for advertising, banking, and so on.
- **Coverage**: If an individual is ill or has an otherwise personal issue, which means they need to step away from the work, then others in the cooperative can step in.
- **Financial security:** As a freelancer, you are very exposed if something happens, like a client refuses to pay. As a cooperative, you can pool some money as a safety net to help out with those sorts of situations.

Having insurance specific to their work as freelancers is a concept some might not be aware of. What type of insurance does Talespinners have, and how does it benefit the members of the co-op?

Every creative freelancer who contributes to a project should have indemnity insurance, i.e., insurance that protects you if your client is sued in a way that means they try to get damages out of *you*, citing your work as being at fault. Many clients will insist on you having a certain level of indemnity insurance in the contract you sign with them. Even if they don't, it's safest to have it (you can get a blanket policy) to protect yourselves. This applies whether you're an individual or a company. It's much cheaper for a group of people in a company to get that insurance, rather than for a set of different individuals. As an example, Talespinners is protected up to claims of a million GBP.

How does Talespinners market itself to prospective clients?

Talespinners presents itself as an outsource writing studio that consists of a number of skilled and experienced writers and designers with a very wide range of different disciplines, skill sets, and genres, capable of taking on a wide variety of tasks. The company is a one-stop solution to a client's narrative headaches!

How does Talespinners determine everyone's responsibilities or who will be assigned to certain projects?

There is no magic formula here—it very much depends from project to project. Who gets which piece of work will depend on who brought the work to the company, who has the best-fit skill set, who *wants* that piece of work most, and who *needs* that piece of work most. As time has gone on, it's actually less about "who doesn't have any work!" and has become more "who has time for this one!"

What advice would you give to anyone who might be considering starting a freelance co-op or partnership?

Just do it! It is infinitely better than working on your own. With that, though, a few caveats—set some ground rules on who is going to do things like admin and invoicing (and make sure their time is compensated somehow), and make sure the general rules of the partnership or co-op are written down, particularly when it comes down to how any money is going to be split from any income. It avoids future arguments. Oh, and make sure the people you are going into business with are actually good at their work and that you can trust them, otherwise there is a danger that you will end up doing the lion's share and effectively carrying someone else, which will not help your stress levels!

Talespinners has also worked with subcontractors. Why is hiring subcontractors something freelancers should consider?

Talespinners initially called in freelancers either when hit by too much work at once, or when it needed to call in a skill set that wasn't in the core company. It is useful for several of the reasons we've discussed above—and in particular, it makes life very simple for the clients. If, for example, they suddenly say, "We need to double the amount of writing for the next couple of months," then they can rely on Talespinners to do that, to find freelancers that the rest of us as writers trust and who we know will fit into a team seamlessly. From the client's point of view, finding more writers to work alongside Talespinners temporarily would be extremely tricky.

Working with subcontractors is also a good way to spread work around to other people you like and trust in the industry. And, who knows, perhaps one day they'll be part of the cooperative, too—that's certainly how Talespinners initially grew, from people Giles and I had already outsourced work to.

What advice would you give to freelancers who might be interested in hiring subcontractors?

Hire people you know you can trust and who will fit in with your house style. And don't screw them out of money! Treat them as you would want to be treated. "Rebadging" someone else's work as your own is not the way to go here. Which is another thing to bear in mind—Talespinners has standard contracts in place with clients, which insist on proper credits for everyone involved, and as a company, it's much easier to achieve that.

TAXES AND LAWS FOR FREELANCERS

Where you live will also affect *what* you pay and *when* you pay it. Before I set up my LLC, I talked with a lawyer and did some additional research about my legal responsibilities. Still, I kept discovering more and more fees I had to pay and information I had to report. I had no clue I had to pay personal property tax every year or that I needed a business license. Sometimes, you don't know what you need to do or look up unless someone informs you.

I have a single-member LLC. In the United States, each state has different laws for LLCs incorporated in the state. In New Mexico, business owners pay a one-time fee to set up their LLC. They only pay yearly state taxes if their LLC made money *within the state of New Mexico*, plus federal taxes. In Tennessee, business owners pay a one-time fee to set up their LLC; yearly state, county, and city business taxes based on the types of services the LLC offers; a yearly annual report (starting at $300, more if there is more than one owner); franchise and excise tax (minimum $100, and based on how much the LLC made in state); and property taxes covering equipment, plus federal taxes. See why it's important to know what you must pay and when?

What Must You Report?

You have to report yearly income from your freelance business. Depending on where you are, when you send payments is also critical.

To find relevant forms for filing your taxes, go to your tax agency's website.

Earnings

These are what you make as a freelancer every year.

Value-Added Tax (European Union and United Kingdom)

This is a very brief overview of value-added tax (VAT). By all accounts, VAT is very complex. So, if this applies to you, please consult with a tax professional about it.

Individuals buying the service pay for the VAT. VAT-registered businesses act as tax collectors and pass the VAT on to the government (the VAT is a percentage added on top of the rate for the service). Depending on what country you're in, your business has to make a certain amount every year to meet a VAT threshold. Once that threshold is met, your business is legally required to register as a VAT business. You can also register as a VAT business without meeting the threshold.[10] The benefit of being a VAT-registered business is that you can claim your business expenses over the course of a year and get a VAT refund on new equipment, like a laptop or printer.[11]

Quarterly Payments or Estimated Tax (United States)

In the United States, whether you're a sole proprietor or have an LLC, you must make quarterly payments. These are also referred to as estimated tax because you're *estimating* how much taxable income you've made each quarter.

Quarters By Dates:

First Quarter: January 1–March 31 (Payment due by April 15)

Second Quarter: April 1–May 31 (Payment due by June 15)

Third Quarter: June 1–August 31 (Payment due by September 15)

Fourth Quarter: September 1–December 31 (Payment due mid-January)[12,13,14]

How do you calculate your estimated tax? A good rule of thumb a CPA[15] told me is to multiply what you've made in a quarter by 20%.

> If you make $5000.00 from June 1 to August 31, your estimated tax is $1000.00:
>
> $$\$5000.00 \times .2 = \$1000.00$$

What if you miss one of your quarterly payments? That's okay, *as long as you pay all of your estimated taxes by the last quarterly date.* According to 2021 Form 1040-ES Estimated Tax for Individuals, "You do not have to make the [fourth quarter] payment if you file your... tax return by January 31...**and** pay the entire balance due with your return."[16]

What happens if you don't make your quarterly payments or underpay? Well, you'll be penalized when you file your yearly return.

This is why *you must report what you paid in estimated taxes on your tax return.* If you don't do your own taxes, make sure you include this information for your CPA or tax preparer. Don't assume the IRS is going to magically remember this on your behalf.

How do I know? The very first year I made quarterly payments, my tax preparer had finished inputting all of the information I had given him into the software. He told me what I owed the IRS, including the penalty for not paying estimated tax.

"But I paid that!" I said incredulously, and told him how much.

"Oh, well, let me add that in!" And he inputted the amount. Voilà! The form no longer said I would be assessed a penalty, and I now owed very little.

Your Payments to Subcontractors

When you hire and work with subcontractors (or maybe you've hired free-lancers to work on your own projects), you also must report how much you paid them. Again, depending on where you live, this might require more than one form and specific dates by when you need to report those payments.

In the United States, you're required to send this information to both the IRS and the subcontractor. The subcontractor also has to have this information in order to report their earnings to the IRS or tax agency in their country.

The IRS has Form 1099-NEC, for nonemployee compensation. You send Copy B of this form directly to the subcontractor, while Copy C is the payer's (you) filing included with your tax returns.

KEEP A RECORD OF YOUR EXPENSES

Keeping good records of your expenses not only gives you an accurate account of how much you spend on your business in a year, but it can also cut into what you owe in taxes every year through deductions. The follow-ing sections cover some expenses you can claim as deductions.

What Do You Spend on Your Business?

You can claim all of the following on your tax returns in the United States (if you are not in the United States, please research what you can and can't claim!). I'll start with the more costly items.

Conferences and Conventions

Speaking at and attending conferences and conventions are seen as part of your professional development. Freelancers are allowed to include bet-tering themselves for business success on their taxes. There are several expenses connected to attending conferences and conventions. How much you can claim is sometimes limited to a daily amount, like how much you can claim on meals in a day:

- Attendance cost: What you pay for the badge, pass, or ticket.

- Meals: What you pay for breakfast, lunch, and dinner each day.

- Travel: Your ticket to get to the event, whether by air, train, or bus.

- Hotel: Your hotel fees.

- Rideshare, public transportation: Anything you have to pay to get around the area.

Equipment

You should claim whatever equipment you buy in a given year to use as a part of your business. Note that you might also have to report the value of your equipment every year if you are responsible for paying personal property taxes[17]:

- Laptop and or desktop computer: These are not cheap, and you're reliant on them for everything from playing builds, producing documents, sending e-mails, and communicating over platforms like Slack and Discord.

- Printers and multifunction centers (MFCs): Your equipment for printing and scanning in your home office.

- Gaming consoles and peripherals: Don't forget to include these! Even if you're not playing your clients' builds on these, playing games is integral to understanding games, your work, and the player's experience.

- Software: Claim what you use in conjunction with your laptop or desktop to do your job. This can include the Adobe Suite, Office 365, antivirus programs, etc.

Your Taxes and Fees for Permits and Licenses

Yes, these count! As do the expenses for paying for a CPA's or tax preparer's services.

Services and Subscriptions

Include any services you use in your business. These are going to be as diverse and unique to the individual business. Here are some of the services you might pay for:

- Cloud Storage: If you save any of your clients' work on the cloud, include this as an expense.

- Training Courses: These can be anything that advance your professional development, like Udemy courses, master classes, etc.

- Video Conferencing: Claim if you pay for Zoom or other services.

- Project Management Systems and Platforms: These include monthly or annual subscriptions to Basecamp, Freedcamp, Notion, Trello, etc.

- Streaming Services: Netflix, Hulu, Disney+, etc., are legitimate services for a freelancer to claim, especially when you're a writer. They provide stories that you can analyze and learn from to improve your writing craft.

- VPNs: Include this as an expense if you use a VPN on a laptop or desktop on which you work.

- Internet and Wi-Fi: Claim what you pay every year for your Internet service.

- Cell phone: Claim what you pay every year for your phone services.

Professional Development

I mentioned attending conferences is part of a freelancer's professional development. It's expected that professionals will continue to work on their skills, and they must pay out of pocket to do so. In some industries, individuals are *required* to do a certain amount of professional development over a period of time, or they could lose their certification(s) or licenses.

Other types of learning materials:

- Language training

- Educational materials

- Games, comics/manga, films, music, etc.: Yes! These count! They're not just forms of entertainment. Since you're working with a storytelling medium in games, playing, reading, watching, or listening to stories helps you learn about them and become a better storyteller.

Lunch or Dinner Meetings

If you pay for business meetings at lunch or dinner, claim these. Again, you may only be able to claim up to a certain amount or percentage of what you spent overall in this area.

Office Supplies

- Printing paper

- Mailing envelopes

- Stamps

- Writing implements

- Erasers

- Staplers

- Paperclips, etc.

Talk to Your CPA/Tax Preparer!

If you don't know what you can and can't claim, ask your tax preparer about it. It's better to keep track of too much than not enough, or having no record of some things that could reduce what you owe.

Record Keeping

Spreadsheets and Word Processors

There's the old, clichéd story of people throwing all of their receipts and other documents into a shoebox, which they carry to their tax preparer. Freelancers live out a kind of digital version of this, with e-mails for their receipts, e-mails, and messages where they've attached invoices to be paid by their clients, and messages and notifications tracking possible tax deductions. Spreadsheet and Word templates can help you track all deductions and taxable income. If you do a quick search online, you can find one that suits your organizational style and that you find easy to use. One such example is here: https://sixcolors.com/post/2017/03/freelance-accouting-template-the-2017-edition/.

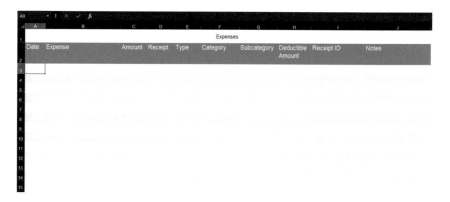

The accounting spreadsheet template from the Six Colors website. This version was converted from a numbers spreadsheet to an Excel spreadsheet.

If you're adept at programming spreadsheets, you can make a template that suits your needs.

But receipts and invoices can stack up over a year, and keeping track of them can get intimidating. There's an additional problem with receipts: The ink printed on them can degrade quickly; in a few months, you may not be able to read them anymore. This can be a real problem when you're trying to add up how much you've spent over the year or input it into a spreadsheet. (And, let's be honest, how many of us immediately add our expenses to a spreadsheet or other rolling tab as soon as we've spent the money?)

There are a couple of ways to keep a handle on this, so you're not flailing and trying to find all of your relevant receipts or payment information.

Keeping Track of Your Receipts, Invoices, and Payments

There are mobile apps designed specifically for record keeping, as they scan and track your physical documents. They're easy to use because they take pictures of physical receipts and invoices through your phone's camera. (I have also used them to take laptop screenshots of e-mails!) These apps include Smart Receipts, Expensify, Shoeboxed, and Veryfi.[18]

You can arrange your receipts into categories, like services, client invoices, etc., and they keep a running tally on your expenses and payments received.

Categorize Your E-Mails

Gmail has a label system, which makes it very easy to find and save e-mails. I have been using labels for years. I have labels for things like each client I have worked with, fiction submissions, payments I've received from clients, and receipts to track my expenses. As soon as I receive an e-mail, I label it. I can then go back to that label and find all those relevant e-mails. It's an effective digital filing system.

If you don't use Gmail, your mail folders can work in a similar way. Name folders for however you want to categorize your e-mails, and move your e-mails to those folders for record keeping.

SHOULD YOU GET INSURANCE?

Freelancers can find themselves in legal troubles, like being hit with copyright infringement, defamation, libel and slander, and errors and omission suits. Insurance is available to both freelancing individuals and companies and protects against such suits. If you're in the United States, you will also need to consider paying for your own health, vision, and dental insurance. And, if you're responsible for dependents, you will have to pay for their insurance, as well.

Types of Insurance for Freelancers

Freelancers can find themselves subjected to lawsuits. It's highly unusual for a client to extend liability coverage to freelancers.[19] Therefore, you're going to need to protect yourself. Just what you pay in legal fees for representation—not to mention what you'd have to pay should you be found liable—can be exorbitant.

Here are the types of insurance to consider for you and your business. Again, availability for coverage will depend on where you live.

Indemnity

Contracts can contain indemnity clauses. In an indemnity clause, any harm or damage, intentional or unintentional, caused to a party transfers from one contractual party to another:

> An indemnity clause is a promise by one party (the indemnifying party) to be responsible for and cover the loss of the other party (the indemnified party) in circumstances where it would be unfair for the indemnified party to bear the loss. In this way, an indemnity clause is a risk management tool.[20]

In other words, the contractual parties are you and your client. The damaged party can be one of the contractual parties or a third party. For example, if someone claims that the content you wrote caused them harm or damage, then according to the indemnity clause, your client is not responsible for compensating the injured third party—*you are*. This happened to journalist Dolia Estevez in 2013. Estevez wrote that a spokesperson for the Mexican president was one of the "most corrupt Mexicans of 2013" for *Forbes's* website. The spokesperson sued both Estevez and *Forbes* for defamation. The spokesperson also sued Estevez for "intentional infliction of emotional distress" and "interference with business relations."[21] Had Estevez been an employed staff writer, *Forbes* would have defended her[22] and paid for her legal defense. Instead, Estevez' freelance contract with *Forbes* stated that "web writers are 'responsible for any legal claims arising' from their work."[23] The case against Estevez was dismissed, but *Forbes* could have made her responsible for any damages or costs it had to pay.[24]

In software and software adjacent industries like games, the indemnity clause might say that if the freelancer infringes on a third party's intellectual property rights, the client cannot be held responsible. Or the freelancer must pay the client damages if the freelancer infringes on the client's IP rights.

Errors and Omissions

Similar to indemnity, parties may claim that a freelancer caused them losses or damages due to the freelancer making a mistake in their work, the freelancer missing a deadline, or the work being inaccurate. Errors and omissions insurance (E&O) protects your business against these lawsuits.[25]

Business Interruption Insurance

Business interruption insurance (BII) covers loss of income should your normal operations be interrupted by a natural disaster or damage to property where you work.[26] Many telecommuting freelancers work at home, but if you rent a space and that space is damaged, consider getting BII.

Health, Dental, and Vision Insurance

If you're in the United States or another country that doesn't have publicly funded health care, your clients will not provide your health care coverage, as they would for their employees. Taking care of your physical and mental health is essential for your life in general, and it can be difficult to work (or even look for work) if you're dealing with health issues and can't attend to them. I speak as someone who's had experience with dental problems popping up from time to time, even though I take good care of my teeth. If I were not able to address those issues early, I would have been hampered by pain and fatigue. Having dental insurance, knowing I would have a percentage of my bills paid for, allowed for me to attend to my teeth immediately. While going to appointments disrupted my schedule, there would have been days at a time where I would not have been productive.

Should health problems arise (God forbid) for you or someone who is dependent on you, you'll want to be able to see a doctor and not worry about not having insurance.

DO I NEED INSURANCE? CHECKLIST

1. Research types of insurance you need for your business.
2. Compare plans specifically for freelancers/independent contractors and costs.

CONTRACTS AND CLAUSES

Contracts are a must. They are the legally binding documentation that protects both you and your client should anything go wrong with your project. Or should either party be unclear on your job, you can always point to the contract.

NEVER start a job without a legally binding contract in place. In the following section, I'll cover the contracts you'll most likely be executing as a freelancer and the kinds of clauses and language to include in your contracts to benefit you.

WORK-FOR-HIRE AGREEMENTS

If you or your client is in Japan, the United Kingdom, the United States, or Australia, you will most likely have a work-for-hire contract. Under a work-for-hire agreement, the client will own all rights to any content you produce. This kind of contract might take getting used to for writers who sell their short stories and novels to publishers or prose fiction markets—those markets will obtain rights to publish your work, but they don't end up owning the rights to your stories. You have to change your perspective when it comes to work-for-hire gigs. By the end of your time on the project, you will not have a say in how the content you've created is disseminated, or if it will even be used.

How does work-for-hire law work with some countries' copyright laws? In certain countries, once you write down a tangible idea—even if it's on the corner of a napkin—you will own the rights to that idea. The work-for-hire contract establishes an agreement between freelancer and client that the rights for those ideas will transfer to the client. In other words, you hand over those rights to the client. (More on that in a moment.)

Some clients, especially established ones, will have their own work-for-hire contracts. Other clients may ask if you have a contract template that you like to use, and you will then negotiate clauses that go into the template.

INTERVIEW WITH FRED WAN: THE LAWYER

Fred Wan is a trial lawyer by day, and narrative designer and diversity consultant by night in both tabletop and digital spaces. His main areas of focus are giving players more ways to engage with and impact game worlds and each other, and using mechanics and narrative to strengthen each other. His best-known work was over a decade as one of the Story Leads for the tabletop brand Legend of the Five Rings, published by the Alderac Entertainment Group (now owned by Fantasy Flight Games).

What's a business or legal issue that freelancers often overlook, but it's imperative for them to understand?

The fact that you have legally enforceable rights is separate from actually going ahead and having those rights enforced. Legal actions are expensive—you want to set things up in advance, so none of the parties involved needs to go that route.

Most freelancers will be executing work-for-hire agreements with their clients. Are there other contracts freelancers should be familiar with? When might they use them?

There is one other major one—in some cases, even though you are mentally a freelancer most of the time, your current client might want to outright hire you as an employee for a short-term contract. So, straight employment contracts—and what rights you might have as an employee—are very relevant.

In reviewing this chapter, you noted that accountants can be a better option when freelancers need advice on tax law, and accountants are experts in this area. Are there other matters where seeking the expertise of an accountant over an attorney might be to a freelancer's advantage?

If you want someone to tell you what (specifically) to do in a routine tax situation, "Which receipts do I need to keep?" or "Which form do I have to fill out? These are all so confusing," generally, accountants deal on a day-to-day basis with the infrastructure of the tax system more than a tax lawyer does. It does vary from place to place and on which specific person (accountant or lawyer) you are dealing with.

I also note that accountants are not inexpensive—it's just that in some cases an accountant might be more familiar with certain parts of the tax system, which means they can get it done faster than a tax lawyer. And both usually charge by the hour.

CONTRACT TEMPLATES

Always, always, always, *always* have a signed (that means signed by both you *and* your client), executed contract before you begin any work. Contracts protect both parties and establish what the parties' legal and creative responsibilities are toward the project. If you don't have a contract, you're vulnerable to manipulation, and you won't be able to take legal action against a client should they not meet their obligations.

Don't worry about trying to write up your own contract or having a lawyer draft one for you, which could be expensive. You will find plenty of work-for-hire templates online with a simple search. Once you find a couple that you like, you can ask a lawyer to review them to see if there's anything you should add or remove, based upon your needs.

What to Include in Your Contracts

Your contract needs to clearly state a few things. If your client has their own contract they want to use, negotiate to get these things added if they're not already present.

Your Rate

If you're being paid an hourly, daily, or weekly rate, have this in writing in your contract. State the kind of rate and the amount.

Project Milestones

Milestones are for contracts with flat fees. You and your client agree upon a certain price for all of the work. You then split up that fee among milestones. For example, you and your client agree that you will be paid $10,000. You will get $2500 up-front (an up-front fee or payment). You then have three more payment milestones of $2500 each.

THE UP-FRONT FEE[27]

For my jobs with a flat rate, I charge an up-front fee, especially for jobs that last more than a week. It's a percentage of the overall fee for the job. This is also a milestone payment. Good, serious clients have no problem with you asking for this. It's standard practice. Up-front payment is a retainer for your services and reserves time on your schedule. When you ask for an up-front payment and clients don't balk, you know those clients are serious and professional, and they'll treat you as a professional.

But the up-front payment is also a way of protecting yourself. Sometimes, you get a weird vibe from prospective clients, and you might be concerned that they'll try to not pay you. Or they might have every intention of paying, but they might lose their funding or go overbudget on another project. Projects fall through for all sorts of reasons beyond the client's control. The up-front payment makes these clients you're not sure about bleed a little. They're sacrificing something to prove they're serious, and you won't be left with nothing.

You could wait to be paid the entire sum at the end of the project, but I would highly recommend *against* this, unless the project is under a couple of weeks.

Nonpayment Milestones

Also include performance milestones. These are for when you will deliver work to the client. It's best if you specify the exact date when these milestones are due. If the schedule should change, you and your client can always renegotiate milestone dates.

Your client should have milestones, too! Note by what date the client will return feedback to you. If you don't get feedback from your client in a certain amount of time, you will not be able to deliver your work by agreed-upon deadlines. Client milestones make it clear to them that they are also responsible for making sure you produce content they'll be pleased with.[28]

Revision Milestones

Have specific milestones for when you will deliver revisions (first, second, final, etc.).

When You're Paid

It's not enough to note how much you'll be paid. Document when you'll be paid, whether that's every two weeks, at the end of the month, weekly, or a specific milestone date. If you're sending your client invoices, make sure you do so in time, so you don't delay any payments.

How You're Paid (and Who Pays You)

And it's not enough to note how much you'll be paid and when you'll be paid. You also need to say *how* you'll be paid. This might be a direct deposit to your checking account or a PayPal payment. Be sure your client has the right information (your bank info, the e-mail address for your PayPal account, etc.), and make sure you know who on the client's side is responsible for paying you, whether that's the individual(s) you're in direct contact with or someone in another department. You need to know whom to contact in the event that you have to track down a missing payment.

Want to know how excruciatingly painful it can be if you do not indicate how you'll be paid? Please see Chapter 14, "Please Learn from My Ignorance."

Not having all the specifics around how much, when, and how you're paid can lead to confusion over your payments and delays.

The Number of Revisions

State exactly how many revisions are included in the contract. (I like to include two.) If your client needs more revisions, you can negotiate how many and for what cost. Additional revisions should cost more, since they weren't a part of the original contract.

Limiting your revisions causes your client to give you more focused and detailed feedback, and it keeps you from doing endless revisions. Some scam or manipulative clients will keep freelancers doing endless revisions. It's a way to get free content, and they never have to pay because they're not "satisfied." This isn't always done out of malice; the client is unaware of how time consuming this is or that it's impeding your ability to take on more work.

How You Will Be Credited

Have in writing exactly how you will be credited in-game and in other published materials. Fighting for credits can be an exhausting process. (This is a ridiculous fight, by the way. If you contributed, you should receive recognition, just like any other dev who worked on the project.) Getting your client to agree in the contract that you *will be* credited is an important step to making sure your name and recognition for your work actually make it into the finished game.

This clause should include your name, your business (if you want it in the credits), and your role. Make sure each is spelled correctly and is written exactly as you want it to appear.

Clauses to Protect You from Scope Creep

Scope creep happens when you end up doing work outside the scope you and your client agreed to. In other words, you're doing additional work you're not getting paid for. This usually happens when the client asks if you can do *one more little thing* or keeps asking for revisions. That *one more little thing* can turn into *ten more little things* if you're not careful.

Scam clients will abuse scope creep, while other clients don't realize they're asking you for extra work and that you should be paid for doing it.

Saying exactly what your work entails, having clearly defined duties and responsibilities for both you and your client, and including milestones (if you're getting a flat fee) will help against scope creep. But you also need anti-scope-creep language that will protect you. State that in a clause that if additional work is needed, you can negotiate a new rate with your client.

A VERY IMPORTANT CLAUSE[29]

Back to work-for-hire agreements for a moment. This is for anyone working in countries with work-for-hire copyright laws. In the United States, as soon as you put an idea down in a tangible form, you own the idea. If I write three words on a napkin, I own the copyright to those three words.[30] With work-for-hire jobs, you *must* assign the rights to someone else, even if you're creating content for them. Otherwise, the rights stay with you, and you should be making some kind of payment agreement for the client to continue to use your work (which is an unusual arrangement in freelancing). So, make sure you have a clause in your contract that assigns rights to the client, and make sure that the clause protects you.

If you say something like "all rights will transfer upon final payment," it will behoove your client to make sure you're paid *IN FULL*. That final payment milestone is the last one listed in your contract, after you have completed all of the work and received the rest of your agreed-upon payments. If that final payment does not happen, you will remain the copyright owner of the content you produce.

WHEW! THAT WAS A LOT…

This chapter provides a lot of things for you to research and implement into your own business. The goal was not to make this seem like a daunting task, but I did want to impress upon you that there's a *lot* that goes into establishing a business, and there are some things you absolutely must do to protect yourself and keep your business running legally.

EXERCISES

Claiming Deductions

Make a list of all of the potential deductions you can claim on your taxes. These can include:

- conference and convention fees (and the hotel, travel, and meals for these conferences),
- business equipment,
- training courses or classes,
- professional development,
- games, etc.

Contract Review

Review any contract templates you're already using.

1. Are you missing any clauses or information covered in this chapter?
2. Add these missing clauses to your contract templates.

NOTES

1. I do want to thank Fred Wan for reviewing this chapter and making sure I had the legal stuff straight.
2. Julie Davoren, "What Is the Difference between Incorporated & Unincorporated Businesses?," *Houston Chronicle*, last modified January 28, 2019, https://smallbusiness.chron.com/difference-between-incorporated-u nincorporated-businesses-57463.html.
3. Julie Davoren, "What Is the Difference between Incorporated & Unincorporated Businesses?," *Houston Chronicle*, last modified January 28, 2019, https://smallbusiness.chron.com/difference-between-incorporated-u nincorporated-businesses-57463.html.

4. Julie Davoren, "What Is the Difference between Incorporated & Unincorporated Businesses?," *Houston Chronicle*, last modified January 28, 2019, https://smallbusiness.chron.com/difference-between-incorporated-u nincorporated-businesses-57463.html.

5. Scott Edward Walker, "Ask the Attorney: The Pros and Cons of Single-Member LLCs," Venturebeat, last modified February 1, 2010, https://venturebeat.com/2010/02/01/ask-the-attorney-the-pros-and-cons-of-single-member-llcs/.

6. "Co-Op Mastery: Beyond Cooperatives 101," Ohio State University, accessed November 11, 2021, https://u.osu.edu/coopmastery/legal/alterna-tive-business-structures/.

7. "Choose Your Business Structure: Cooperative," Tony Burch Foundation, accessed November 11, 2021, http://www.toryburchfoundation.org/resources/starting-a-business/choose-your-business-structure-cooperative-2/.

8. "Choose Your Business Structure: Cooperative," Tony Burch Foundation, accessed November 11, 2021, http://www.toryburchfoundation.org/resources/starting-a-business/choose-your-business-structure-cooperative-2/.

9. "NDA" stands for "non-disclosure agreement." Parties who sign an NDA agree that the sensitive information they discuss and work with will not be shared publicly. Many game projects are under NDA until they are announced publicly.

10. Dan Heelan, "VAT FOR BUSINESS EXPLAINED!," Heelan Associates, July 14, 2021, video, 8:28, https://www.youtube.com/watch?v=82wUl7szBPI.

11. "Benefits of Being VAT Registered as a Freelancer," *Tapoly* (blog), accessed November 11, 2021, https://blog.tapoly.com/benefits-of-being-vat-regis-tered-as-a-freelancer/.

12. "Estimated Tax," IRS.gov, accessed January 17, 2021, https://www.irs.gov/faqs/estimated-tax.

13. Form 1040-ES, U.S. Department of the Treasury, Internal Revenue Service (Washington, DC, 2021), https://www.irs.gov/pub/irs-pdf/f1040es.pdf.

14. Due dates can fluctuate due to a number of circumstances. Check the IRS website.

15. "CPA" stands for "certified public accountant." They are licensed accounting professionals.

16. Form 1040-ES, U.S. Department of the Treasury, Internal Revenue Service (Washington, DC, 2021), https://www.irs.gov/pub/irs-pdf/f1040es.pdf.

17. Personal property tax: You can be taxed a percentage of the appraised value of the equipment you use in your business. The local or state government determines how the value is appraised.

18. Nadav Elyada, "Top 8 Receipt Scanning Apps You Can't Ignore," Welly Box, last modified September 2, 2020, https://www.wellybox.com/blog/top-7-receipt-scanning-apps/.

19. "Why Freelance Writers (Really) Need Liability Insurance," Freelancersunion.org, last modified October 22, 2020, https://blog.free-lancersunion.org/2020/10/22/why-freelance-writers-really-need-liability-insurance/.

20. "Don't Get Us Started on Indemnity Clauses," Stephenson Law, last modified April 19, 2021, https://www.stephenson.law/dont-get-us-startedon-indemnity-clauses/.

21. Dawn Fallik and Jonathan Peters, "Indemnity Clauses Leave Freelancers Open to Lawsuits," Poynter, last modified May 1, 2015, https://www.poynter.org/reporting-editing/2015/indemnity-clauses-leave-freelancers-open-to-lawsuits/.

22. Dawn Fallik and Jonathan Peters, "Indemnity Clauses Leave Freelancers Open to Lawsuits," Poynter, last modified May 1, 2015, https://www.poynter.org/reporting-editing/2015/indemnity-clauses-leave-freelancers-open-to-lawsuits/.

23. Dawn Fallik and Jonathan Peters, "Indemnity Clauses Leave Freelancers Open to Lawsuits," Poynter, last modified May 1, 2015, https://www.poynter.org/reporting-editing/2015/indemnity-clauses-leave-freelancers-open-to-lawsuits/.

24. Laura Spinney, "How News Publications Put Their Legal Risk on Freelancers," *Columbia Journalism Review*, last modified April 28, 2021, https://www.cjr.org/analysis/freelance-liability-risk.php.

25. "What Is Errors and Omissions Insurance?," Insureon.com, accessed November 11, 2021, https://www.insureon.com/small-business-insurance/errors-omissions.

26. Team Tse, "When You Are Self-Employed, What Insurance Do You Really Need?," last modified June 9, 2015, https://www.theselfemployed.com/when-you-are-self-employed-what-insurance-do-you-really-need/.

27. Adapted from Toiya Kristen Finley, "Freelancing in Games: Narrative Mercenaries for Hire," in *The Advanced Game Narrative Toolbox*, edited by Tobias Heussner (Boca Raton: CRC Press, 2019), 179–201.

28. Sometimes, clients don't realize that they really *do* need to give you feedback. They get the mindset that they can give you a brief, and you will go off for a month or two and write exactly what they're looking for, as if by osmosis or telepathy. Then, after they haven't given you any input, they are shocked to find that you've turned in something they were not expecting. When they are responsible for giving you feedback, both clients and you will know that you're on the right track.

29. Adapted from Toiya Kristen Finley, "Freelancing in Games: Narrative Mercenaries for Hire," in *The Advanced Game Narrative Toolbox*, edited by Tobias Heussner (Boca Raton: CRC Press, 2019), 179–201.

30. Betsy Rosenblatt, "Copyright Basics," Harvard.edu, last modified March, 1998. https://cyber.harvard.edu/property/library/copyprimer.html.

CHAPTER 9

How to Get Experience If You Don't Have It

How many times has this happened to you? A post for a writing gig shows up in your Facebook feed or on Twitter. It's a fun project. Awesome developer. You feel confident (and that doesn't always happen when you see an ad) that you can do a great job. You click on the link to get more information. On the developer's website, you read the requirements for the ideal candidate.

Talent for writing spoken dialogue.

Check!

Familiarity with Very-Niche-But-Very-Beloved IP?

You betcha!

Shipped at least three titles?

Um…*Well…*

It's the "shipped x number of titles" or "x numbers of years in the industry" that usually trips up otherwise-qualified candidates. It's both disheartening and discouraging to know that you could be a good fit *only if you had the experience.*

DOI: 10.1201/9781003199779-11

I used to think I was stymied by it. In the online groups I'm a part of, I've seen writer after writer virtually bang their heads against the wall when someone posts an opportunity that's perfect for them except for that darn experience issue. And, sometimes, those requirements are intentionally listed as hurdles to see how many people will actually jump over them, whether they're "qualified" or not. It causes would-be applicants to self-disqualify. If you're interested and meet most of the criteria, *apply anyway.*

A lack of experience isn't as great as a hurdle or as big as an obstacle as it may seem to you right now. If you can set aside a little time each week to work on your own projects, you'll have the experience clients are looking for.

And you probably already have some pretty good experience, even though you don't yet recognize it.

This chapter will give you some pointers on how you can start to gain experience right now, even if you've never worked on a game. We'll wrap up the chapter discussing how you can hone the skills devs will find important and avoid nonpaying projects that will waste your time.

WHY'S EXPERIENCE SO IMPORTANT?

There's a pretty good reason why the experience albatross plays such a huge role in job descriptions. In one way, it's a gatekeeping method. Plenty of people—including those who are unqualified in any number of areas—will ignore prerequisites and apply anyway. One of the most eye-opening bits of advice I ever got was when I applied for a job I didn't think I could get because I didn't have enough titles or years under my belt.

A friend referred me for the job. When I told him why I wasn't qualified, he said to me, "They use those prerequisites to weed people out. They don't really expect everyone to have all of those qualifications."

In another way, the experience issue is a real need the client has: Can you see a project through? Games aren't easy to make—even the small ones. If you've ever tried to make a game with a group that wasn't getting paid, you know how quickly that project can fall apart. Projects with large budgets get canceled all of the time, so much so that you've never heard of most of them. So, when you're a part of a completed project, that tells prospective clients a few things:

- you can endure the unpredictability of a development cycle
- you know what to expect from different stages of game development, and

- you've learned how to collaborate with different personalities and temperaments.

GAUGING YOUR LEVEL OF EXPERIENCE

The first thing you'll want to do is a self-assessment of the level of experience you already have. You may have more relevant work and educational experience in your history than you realize, and it's already to your advantage.

Let's take a look at what qualifies as "experience," and how game developers translate it. Your relevant experience is going to be anything that gives you the skills to be a successful game writer and/or narrative designer. You can acquire this from any aspect of your lived experience.

Educational Background

Here's something to remember about the game industry: It's *young.* ATARI released *PONG* in 1972.[1] That means that many devs who've worked in games did not go to school specifically to learn how to make games. Why is that important? It means that even if you don't have a degree in game design or game development, you might have a degree that gives you important expertise and skills to make games. Game development programs are new, too. Thousands of veterans don't have degrees in games. There *weren't any* degrees in games when they got started.

Writers with a degree in English, literature, creative writing, or other writing-oriented majors have a background in storytelling, narrative, plot structure, character development and characterization, dialogue, themes, subtext, and tropes that others looking to get into game writing and narrative design simply do not have. Because of your studies, you're also aware of types of stories and characters and clichés that are prevalent in fiction. This is valuable because you can find ways to subvert archetypes and clichés, or help the team avoid them all together and come up with more original stories.

(While this book is primarily for narrative types, I would be remiss in noting that artists with art degrees, sound designers with degrees in audio, etc., have this same advantage in their disciplines.)

You'll see a line like "English or similar degree" listed in job qualifications. Even if the prospective client doesn't mention this, remember that it's a huge positive for you, and you should use your educational background as a major selling point.

Working in Adjacent Storytelling Industries

Working in any storytelling media gives you great experience when it comes to preparing you for narrative design and game writing work. As is the case with having an educational background in a narrative-related major, working as a prose writer, comics/manga writer, TV writer, theater writer, or scriptwriter gives you skills and expertise as a storyteller. Video games are a different, more immersive medium, but the fundamentals of good storytelling are the same across all narrative media. If you collaborated on projects, that's a bonus. If you're hired for a gig, you'll be working with at least one other person. When I first started working in the industry, veteran writers would recall horror stories of why studios were wary of working with writers. Writers new to the industry, especially novelists and short fiction writers, weren't used to working with a team and didn't understand how the writing was implemented into a game. They very much had an inflexible "solo" mentality.

You've learned storytelling techniques that you can apply to your game projects. For example, if you've written novellas or novels, you've had to plot the rise and fall of the action and think about where to add dramatic tension and find where to let the reader take a breath. The same is true of a game's main plot or critpath.[2]

As a comics writer, you know what it's like to collaborate with artists. You've had to describe scenes, characters, and locations to help the artist visualize your concepts. The same is true when you work with game artists and animators.

> Have you worked as a writer outside of games?
>
> What storytelling techniques did you learn that you could apply to game writing and/or narrative design?

Think about all of the experience you have as a writer in other media and what skills and knowledge make you qualified to work in games.

Research Skills

One of the most important skills a writer can have is the ability to research, and the ability to sort through all kinds of sources. Quickly evaluating which sources will be useful and which ones to toss aside can save you lots of time (and is important to your time management). It's easy to get lost down an information rabbit hole.

Writers know the value of research. It's important for worldbuilding and creating more believable characters. But it's also important when writing documentation for team members. For example, finding the right artist references improves your character bios. You don't want to pick just any references. If you want to suggest a certain hairstyle to the artist, you don't want to pick images of ones that are similar, but not what you have in mind. Even if you tell the artist, "This is kind of what I'm going for," the artist is going to be using an imperfect reference.

Understanding the value of research, how it's beneficial, and *why* your client needs a good researcher is another selling point when you tout your experience.

Seemingly Unrelated Experience

You never can tell when you'll have something in your background that will make you perfect for a project. It might be a talent, a skill you picked up in a trade unrelated to games, or highly specific knowledge on a subject.

One of my clients needed someone to plot out a story for a YA audience. The main characters were girls playing high school volleyball. It just so happened that I played volleyball in high school, and I was a girl. So, on top of my experience writing for a YA audience and my experience plotting stories, I had the same background as the characters.

Did I ever think my past as a middle and high school volleyball player would ever be relevant to my writing career? Nope. But I jumped at the opportunity when it presented itself, and I made sure the client knew my background in volleyball.

Having this kind of background may not be relevant often, but it can make you a more competitive candidate over freelancers who don't share your background.

MAKE YOUR OWN GAMES

Whether you do or don't know programming or scripting, you can make small games to add to your portfolio. Devs want to know that you can finish a project—they don't care if that game is 80 hours long or 8 minutes long. A credit is a credit.

These days, you have access to several platforms made specifically for narrative-heavy and text-only games. They're made with nonprogrammers in mind.

The added benefit of making games to add to your portfolio is that you have something tangible proving you can pick up some scripting or light coding. Clients will occasionally ask game writers and narrative designers to do light scripting.

Twine

When devs give writers advice to make their own games, they usually mention Twine. Twine (not to be confused with the workspace app) is extremely friendly to noncoders and those with absolutely no programming knowledge. Experienced and inexperienced devs alike use Twine to make choice-based games or prototypes. It's easy to use and has an intuitive interface reminiscent of notes connected by string.

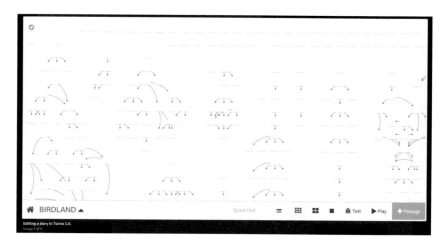

A screenshot of Twine 2.0.

You can quickly pick up how to use conditionals and variables[3]—both foundational to choice-based games—by making short Twine experiences.

David Gaider, a former narrative designer at BioWare, details the importance of learning to use Twine:

It's purely writing-based, it will allow you to wrap your head around the idea of branching and you'll produce something that you can not only show later but which will also demonstrate you've taken the time to learn the simple scripting a program like Twine requires. "I possess enough technical capability to learn how to use a conversation editor" is fantastic and will make you stand out.[4]

You can add sound and art assets if you're scripting savvy, but text is enough to get a few short games into your portfolio. There are plenty of resources to teach you Twine, which you can find on Twinery.org, and there is a wealth of Twine tutorials on YouTube for both versions 1.0 and 2.0.

You might do some research on the versions first and then decide which one you want to learn. It doesn't matter which version you use. Ultimately, you will find one easier or more comfortable than the other.

If you're concerned that prospective clients won't respect your short, text-only Twine games, know that AAA developers like BioWare now *encourage* them in writing applications.

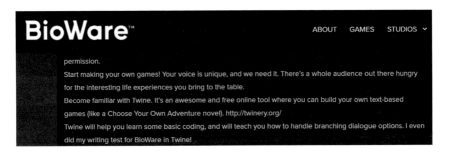

In her "Girls behind Games" interview on BioWare's website, Sam Maggs explains that she used Twine to help get her job at the company.

ink

ink is a narrative scripting language that uses a text-based narrative engine that works in an editor called inky. Like Twine, you can export simple games to the web. ink can also be integrated into Unity projects.

Studios use ink for their choice-based games. *Neo Cab*, *80 Days*, and *Heaven's Vault* were made with ink. Your learning ink can be to your benefit not only because you can add samples to your portfolio, but also because you will learn a scripting language that developers use. If a studio is using ink on a project and you already know it, that's a definite plus for you if you pursue a writing job on that project.

ink's developer, inkle Ltd., has documentation to help you learn ink: https://www.inklestudios.com/ink/. You can also find video tutorials.

ChoiceScript

Choice of Games publishes text-based games. Its ChoiceScript programming language helps writers create choice-based, branching stories and is free to use. Games written in ChoiceScript read like novels, and they track variables (called "stats" by Choice of Games).

ChoiceScript and documentation are available at Choice of Games's website: https://www.choiceofgames.com/make-your-own-games/choicescript-intro/. There are also a variety of ChoiceScript tutorials on YouTube and elsewhere on the web.

Visual Coders

Visual coders (or visual programming languages) allow you to do all of the programming through a graphical interface instead of typing in the code. I'm highly audiovisual, so picking up a language like C++ would take me a long time. However, I can pick up visual coding rather quickly. And visual coders are made specifically to give people the ability to make their own games.

There are several programs available. I'm mentioning a couple here that have plenty of tutorials.

Fungus

I wanted to code my own game for the 2019 Global Game Jam. A few days before it started, I learned Fungus watching tutorial videos in a day and a half and made a fully functional game with sound and art assets that weekend.

Fungus is a Unity add-on, meaning you use it within the Unity engine.

Indie cult favorites *Dream Daddy: A Dad Dating Simulator* and *Purrfect Date: Cat Island* were made in Fungus.

Blueprint

Blueprint is "visual scripting" for the Unreal engine. For documentation, see https://docs.unrealengine.com/4.27/en-US/ProgrammingAndScripting/Blueprints/. There are also plenty of tutorials on YouTube and online elsewhere.

INTERVIEW WITH ELIZABETH LAPENSÉE, PHD

Elizabeth LaPensée, PhD is an award-winning designer, writer, and artist of games, emergent media, and comics. She was named a Guggenheim Fellow in 2018 and inducted into the Global Women in Games Hall of Fame in 2020. She designed When Rivers Were Trails, *a 2D adventure game about land allotment in the 1890s which won the Adaptation Award at IndieCade 2019. She also designed and created art for* Thunderbird Strike, *a lightning-searing side-scroller game which won Best Digital Media at imagineNATIVE Film + Media Arts Festival 2017. She is currently the Lead Writer and World Builder for* Twin Suns.

What led you to pursue freelancing, instead of employment?

I thrive on constant change, new challenges, and building up momentum by completing specific deliverables. Instead of making a company myself or working for a company, my name is effectively my brand. That approach has done well for me for the most part but comes with a huge disclaimer. While there's the benefit of my work being recognizable across whatever I'm working on, the trade-off is that sometimes my name and image get used in unexpected and troubling ways as a target of hate groups. Even when that isn't happening, there's this overwhelming pressure to maintain a presence on social media that I'm in the process of distancing myself from so that I can focus on the part that's fun—the work itself.

My hope is that it doesn't have to be an either/or choice for all of my career. I've recently circled back to a way that long-term employment could work for me—Intellectual Property! I've hesitated to get into IP-style creation because of the fear of losing a say ever since selling a comic script and all of the related IP for $10 early on in my career. All I can pass along from that experience now is to know your worth, even if it's hard for you. Now that I'm in a later phase of my career, I'm returning to IP as a way to both work on the big picture and fine details. I can bounce back and forth between developing a whole universe and hone in on a particular character or fictional backing for a game mechanic. I also have the potential opportunity to delve into different media, such as comics. It gives me the variety I need and keeps me busy enough to feel an ongoing sense of accomplishment.

You're a game writer, but you also work in other disciplines. How many hats do you wear as a game developer?

Uhhh…What needs to get done? I've worked on tasks anywhere from writing dialogue barks to designing mechanics to character art to animation (2D stop motion style) to UI design to worldbuilding. And then some. That's, of course, for smaller-scale games with very little budget that tend to be funded by grants to have just enough support to pay a handful of team members. I've super-appreciated that approach because then the games are available for free, and success is based on how widely they're distributed and how players who the games do reach react. Rather than aiming at numbers, the goal is to create memorable experiences for the players who do come across these games. On large-scale, high-budget games, I stick to writing. With supportive teams, I get to make malleable suggestions regarding design, art, and sound in collaborative contexts while not actually having to implement that work. Having some experience in a variety of tasks does help considerably with communication across the various disciplines on a team. I do my best to adapt to the approaches and lingo across roles, while also recognizing what is and is not possible, so that I'm not throwing big, unfeasible ideas out there as a writer, but rather I'm working closely with everyone in a reciprocal way.

Have you found that your versatility makes you a more attractive candidate for freelancing gigs? Has a client noted your expertise in these areas as a reason for hiring you?

As long as the messaging is clear, versatility can lead to freelance gigs looking for a writer who can cross media as well as provide more opportunities in specific media. While in some instances I've been offered contracts because of work that spans across media, it's really because I specify between media while also having cohesive themes. That's where a well-organized portfolio that shows specific skill sets and also leverages themes is helpful.

I started off my portfolio with specific categories to separate projects out by media, which works well for me in a few ways. It makes it easier for people who are interested in my work to access what they want quickly, which leads to more contract offers. It also gives me goals to strive for and solid direction. For example, if I notice I'm leaning more heavily toward one media category or another, I can take a step back and ask myself if I need to shift focus and balance out my work overall. It also helps me set boundaries that I want to keep for myself, namely that I stick to comics, games, and XR, but not short stories or novels. Every person's choices and categories can and should be different. Just go for what you enjoy most and figure out what limitations you want to set to streamline your focus.

In my case, much of my work tends to interweave back and forth between different media with crossovers in themes. For example, the comic *They Walk as Lightning* in *MOONSHOT Volume 2* ties in with the game *Thunderbird Strike*. This strategy is almost a transmedia approach, but since the characters and places are all different, it focuses on evoking connection and shared meaning, so that when someone visits my work, hopefully they get a strong sense of what it would be like to work with me, whatever media that may happen through. It's really the themes that ignite potential collaborators to reach out to me.

Have you sometimes ended up doing design on a game, when you were only hired to write? Did your client offer to pay you separately for that work?

There's some kind of line here that I'm still trying to figure out because I've definitely been in situations where I've contributed very directly to design and implemented that work myself and not been paid separately for or even credited for it. That can be a huge issue for someone who wants and in fact needs to be seen as a writer and a designer in order to get contracts that reflect their skills. One quick fix is to negotiate a credit from Writer to Narrative Designer, but that still doesn't reflect the full amount of work. Personally, I vary in what title I want on each game, and appreciate when a team is open to discussion and working with me to create our own definition of what that title entails and what that means in terms of paid deliverables.

For me, the ideal is to be able to share perspectives and make suggestions with a team that is open, honest, and values different insights. But then it's the designers who are responsible for final decisions and implementation, not based on their own opinions, but on playtests and collective feedback. When I'm collaborating with designers who listen and work through challenges, it makes my role as a writer more focused and enjoyable. Being clear about limitations (with flexibility in some cases) and working together toward the shared goal of awesome gameplay keeps me going.

You mentioned what credit you want varies. How do you determine how you wish to be credited on a project-by-project basis?

I appreciate companies who are willing to reassess titles based on the work provided throughout a contract. In general, I tend to lean toward "Writer" because it's understandable as a role beyond the game industry. Most recently, I am the Lead Writer and World Builder for *Twin Suns*. If at any point I wanted to switch to Narrative Designer, they're open to that. They suggested the additional World Builder part of the title because they wanted to make sure that the level of depth in the work I am doing is conveyed, which was very considerate of them. Collaborating with a team that looks out for you is key, whatever title you end up advocating for.

You've released your own game. How important is it to work on your own projects to develop your skills and voice as a writer and designer?

Self-expression through games that can be shown at festivals, exhibitions, and events has been key to being able to share what is truest to my voice. I've also designed and directed games like *When Rivers Were Trails* where the emphasis for me was to uplift more voices while I was in a role to facilitate their self-expression. In that instance, there were around 30 writers, which is a whole other conversation! Ha ha. *When Rivers Were Trails* and *Thunderbird Strike* especially stand out for me about what can happen when games are self-determined. I'm grateful that I've been able to work on enough games independently that the difference between self-determination and what happens when there's a wider system at play (often industry expectations and the pressure to make sales).

Having said that, the reality is that I don't have the resources or capacity to direct, design, and write large budget games, so there is a limit on what I'm able to do. So, while I appreciate that I've been able to do what I can by applying for grants or collaborating with partners and with what I can personally invest, I recognize that there's a range of possibilities in game development often based on, well, money. Ideally, I hope to gain experience by also collaborating on larger-scale games with a team that is open to listening and finding ways for all voices to be reflected in their collective work.

You were working on your game while having a day job. What advice do you have for freelancers who need to grow their portfolios but are having difficulty finding the time?

And now for a chronically honest moment! I've struggled to find a balance in life because I had to work very hard to get to where I'm at. For much of my early career, I was just focused on getting by day to day as a single mom working jobs that didn't relate to my ideal path and couldn't be included in my portfolio, like journalism gigs or copyediting or teaching skills like grant writing. I even moved back in with my parents for a bit in order to be able to put most of what I earned into self-funded games and comics. I often worked an average of four to five contracts at a time and never knew when the money would arrive, so I had to keep just enough set aside to make it month to month. For years, I worked through nights and weekends, and that pattern is so ingrained in me that I often fall back into it. I'm just on the cusp of figuring out what needs to be cut back so that I can live in a more balanced way.

Ultimately, working on several small-scale games, comics, and other projects that were more readily completable and could immediately go on my portfolio did work for me. I can now hold out while focusing on games that have turnarounds of three or more years to release and not be worried about proving myself in the meantime since my portfolio is robust. The intensity I put into this approach isn't healthy though, and I'm at a place where it's just not sustainable since I put just as much effort into family and community as work. For a balanced alternative, it may be a matter of either completing fewer smaller-scale games but still having something in circulation in festivals and exhibitions, or patiently working very gradually on a larger-scale game. Whichever path you take, game development involves a lifelong dedication to constant learning and being open to making mistakes in order to work through them.

How has writing and editing comics strengthened your skills as a game writer or given you a new perspective on game storytelling?

By far, comics have been especially transferable to games, both in terms of communicating with teams and deliverables. By having some experience with illustration, I can better understand the process of an art director and other members of an art team (and feel for them when they're turning out sketch after sketch because I get the physicality of it). On the design end, my experience in writing and illustrating comics can be applied to story-boarding out gameplay, which is very helpful for games I'm directing and also applicable when working through the fiction side hand in hand with the work of designers on a larger team. Even when I'm exclusively focused on writing, I often gather reference materials, such as photos or relevant art when writing up characters, or filling in fiction for anything ranging from levels to weapons to gear. If artists and designers go on to gather their own references too, that can become a talking point with a strong foundation of visual support to communicate and work together in ways that feel exciting and tangible.

How can writers use their experience in other media to get video game work?

Think about how those skills you've honed from other media transfer over to video games and specifically focus on those aspects.

How might your previous character creation experience in media of any kind lead to stronger video game characters? If you do write very text-heavy characters with backstories and all, how can you quickly and efficiently communicate the essentials of those characters in keywords or visuals in ways that can reach the entire team you're collaborating with? It's always good practice to see what out of your prior work can be adapted readily to sheets with rows and columns of specific information and/or digital whiteboards that utilize visual communication.

If you write comic scripts, how might that inform key gameplay moments, cutscenes, or attention-grabbing barks? How does writing dialogue within the boundaries of small speech bubbles lend to writing for games with limited word (or even character) counts? How does focusing on action in comics potentially reflect your understanding of mechanics?

Whatever your prior experiences with other media might be, finding ways to show that you can make connections between fiction and game-play is vital in video games.

SKILLS TO SHOWCASE IN YOUR GAMES

When writing projects for your portfolio, make sure that you're intention-ally *illustrating* certain skills to prospective clients—not just making an entertaining game. I don't mean you need to say, "And here is my excellent characterization," but anyone reviewing your work needs to see that you understand what makes for good playing experiences.

The first couple of skills are based on your narrative design abilities, while the second two are aspects of game writing. You can focus on pursuing only game writing or narrative design jobs, but improving and displaying narrative design and game writing skills will give you more opportunities for work.

Choice Design (Narrative Design)

A lot of story-heavy games give players choices. Your portfolio samples should illustrate how you design choices and your understanding for facilitating the player's agency. Choices entail both actions and dialogue options. They need to be clear. Think of the times you've made a choice while playing a game, and you got an unpleasant surprise—the choice expressed the exact *opposite* of what you meant to do or say.

Keep a few things in mind when you're writing choices for your portfolio samples:

- **Avoid giving only one choice.** This is basically a "click-through," or little more than a continue. For example, to advance the story, the player has to eat the apple. The choice reads "Eat the apple." This isn't a real choice because the player isn't making a decision between two or more actions.

- **Avoid synonymous choices.** These are dialogue choices that seem to be suggesting the same sentiment or emotion; they're only worded differently. Or they're choices between actions where the player can't tell the difference between what they'll end up doing.

- **Avoid Hobson's choices.** While there are two or more choices, there's only one real choice: "Do it, or don't."/"Take it, or leave it." The Hobson's choice forces players to choose "Do it" or "Take it." These leave players frustrated because they feel tricked into making a certain choice.

- **Add difficult choices where appropriate for your story.** Difficult choices can be agonizing for players because both options seem great, or both options seem like they'll lead to negative outcomes. These are emotionally engaging.

- **Add choices with immediate and long-term consequences.** When players make a choice, they get immediate feedback, either through an NPC or the story. But the choice also leads to positive or negative consequences that you track through variables. Designing long-term consequences illustrates that you understand variables in branching stories, and it proves to players that their choices are meaningful.

And, remember, the games should *always* respond to the player's choice in some way. NPCs respond directly to the player's dialogue choice, and/or the game tracks a player's decision that influences the story later. Players often feel that their choices don't matter. Show how their choices *absolutely* matter in your game.

Worldbuilding (Narrative Design)

You don't have to have art, animation, or sound assets to effectively world-build. In a text-based game, you can implement worldbuilding through sensory details. Try to incorporate *all* of the senses. Writers tend to focus on sight or what locations, characters, and scenes look like, but hearing, touching, tasting, and smelling are equally as important.

Dialogue Writing (Game Writing)

Think about dialogue as more than just two or more characters responding to each other. While that's important, dialogue can reveal a lot about characters, the world, and even the story.

Think about the *functions* of your dialogue. Use it to

- reveal the characterization of the player-character and NPCs,
- give information about the world,
- foreshadow events, and/or
- give the player clues.

Character Development and Characterization (Game Writing)

Reflect aspects of your characters' personalities and attitudes through their dialogue, actions, and behavior and responses toward the player and other NPCs. This illustrates your understanding of characterization and how you flesh out believable characters.

Make sure that you have some character development for some of your characters. How do you convey how they're changing, for good or ill, throughout the game? How do the arising conflicts and plot developments change or *reveal* who they are?

PARTICIPATE IN GAME JAMS

By participating in game jams, you'll develop collaboration skills while building your portfolio. Game jams are year-round events, and there are plenty occurring online.

The goal of a game jam is to finish a game in a specified period of time. Jams can be a few days, a week, or even a month. Game jams tend to have a theme: Games must be made in a particular engine, they must be made using a particular tool, or they place other constraints upon participants to spark creativity and innovation. Some participate in game jams solo, but most form teams. You collaborate with a team that needs your skills. While you can work with a group where you know everyone, it can also be to your benefit to work with strangers. As a freelancer, you'll most likely be working with new teams all of the time. Working with new people at multiple game jams gets you accustomed to different communication and learning styles and different personalities.

Not finishing a game by the end of a jam is *not* considered a failure. Your participation in the game jam itself is important to note on your résumé/CV. Of course, if you *do* finish a game, you want to add a playable version to your portfolio and highlight your work on it.

 INTERVIEW WITH ROKASHI EDWARDS

Rokashi Edwards (they/them) is a game developer, writer, Sonic the Hedgehog *enthusiast, and certified weirdo. They have a passion for narrative design and love to create games that focus on mental health in order to educate people wherever they go. They are currently creating* Faraway Fairway *for the Playdate console!*

What led you to pursue freelancing, instead of employment?

It was a lot easier for me at the time. I needed more income while working retail, so I hustled to find more opportunities online that I could write, edit, or anything else, and I'd do that while on my full-time retail job break and continue when I got home. The struggle was hard, but I was really dedicated, so I had to continue to push myself further into the industry by any means necessary, and I wasn't going to be taking those "it's for exposure" opportunities—I hate those, and they were definitely not for me. I have bills to pay.

Your first writing job came during a game jam. How did you find that game jam?

It was actually within the Toronto scene, so a lot of people I knew at the time always participated in game jams, but it was something I never really participated in. I was more of a spectator. But the time came when I thought I'd give it a try, and people really enjoyed what I created, so it planted a seed that "Hey, I could be pretty good at this," and it really steered my course on where I wanted to go and what I wanted to do within the scope of video games!

Did you know your jam teammates?

They were kinda strangers to me? No...maybe that's a bit harsh. More so acquaintances. One of them was skilled in creating music, and the other had more experience than me with programming, so me being the writer, it was actually a pretty good small team.

What was it like working with them when you didn't know them?

It was really interesting. I'm kind of introverted, so it was tricky to convey what I wanted to people who were super energetic and outgoing. So, I had to push myself to try to match that kind of energy. The downside was I was exhausted trying to keep up. Even still, I was able to convey the design I was going for, and it worked out in all our favors.

How did the experience prepare you for working in games?

Oh, god. Honestly, I felt like I had a great grasp of what it would be like if I worked on a small indie team creating small games. I think this was slightly before the rise of Itch.io, but I liked it! I don't think I was ready for anything close to creating games at a AAA company like Ubisoft or EA yet, but now? I've learned so much that I think I would excel in that space by combining all that I've experienced.

What opportunities did your jam work bring you? How has having it in your portfolio benefited you?

My game *I'm Fine* was featured in news articles, novels, and premiered at GaymerX and IndieCade. I was traveling and showcasing my game like some sort of professional. I didn't know what the hell was happening. Honestly, I still don't know, but what I do know is that I'm having a great time meeting new people in the industry and gaining the experience I need to make clearer what's next for me.

A lot of people know who I am now, which is weird. I won't say I'm famous or anything, but since my game *I'm Fine* is about mental health, sometimes people confuse my game with Zoe Quinn's *Depression Quest*, which is a fun little thing we both laugh about.

If you were giving advice to someone who's never attended a jam, what are the most important things a first-timer needs to keep in mind?

If there's anyone who wants to try a game jam, the first thing I'd say is to have fun. You're not expected to come out of a jam with the next *Call of Duty* or the next *Grand Theft Auto*. Game jams are a time to just have fun and let your creativity flow while collaborating with others of various disciplines! Also, all forms of games are valid! A simple platformer, a puzzle game, or even a narrative game created in Twine. All are valid forms of play, and don't let people gatekeep you from what a game is.

Where to Find Game Jams

Global Game Jam

The most famous game jam is the Global Game Jam (GGJ), which takes place over a weekend at the end of January every year. As the name suggests, this is an international event with teams on every continent. To participate, you'll need to sign up with a jam site in your area.

For more on the Global Game Jam and to find a site, you can visit GGJ's website: https://globalgamejam.org/.

A team at Nashville, Tennessee's Global Game Jam site in 2020. Photograph by John Gale. ©2020 John Gale

Ludum Dare

Ludum Dare is a biannual game jam taking place every April and October. It's 72 hours. Participants vote on a theme for every jam. Games are reviewed and judged by other participants, and it features a special competition for jammers who want to make a game completely on their own.

More on Ludum Dare is available at https://ldjam.com/.

Other Game Jams

Itch.io users are always running their own game jams. The list is available at https://itch.io/jams. Itch.io makes it easy to join a jam or start your own.

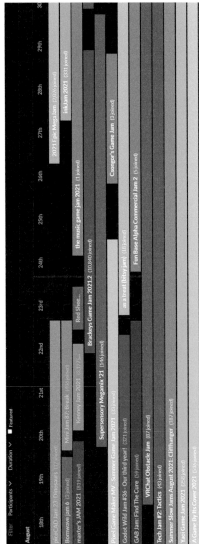

A list of jams hosted by Itch.io users and a calendar listing jams and the number of participants who joined each of them.

Hosts announce their jams on Twitter, Discord, and other social media platforms. Searches should bring up quite a few you can participate in when your schedule allows.

NONPAYING PROJECTS THAT WON'T WASTE YOUR TIME

I believe you should always get some kind of payment for your work. However, there are always teams that are looking for volunteers. Yes, they are opportunities for experience and to have a finished product, but a lot of nonpaying projects aren't worth your time. With a lot of these projects, teams aren't able to properly scope the work *because* they don't have experience. They don't understand how much everyone will have to do. Making games is *hard*. People aren't able to find time when they have day jobs, families, and other commitments.

Developers offer tools to give players the freedom to mod games.

There *are* successful mod teams who've developed projects that the industry respects. *Team Fortress* started as a *Quake* mod. *The Forgotten City* started as a *Skyrim* mod that won several awards.[5]

You can put your own mod team together or join one that needs your skills. When no one is getting paid on the project, you need to make sure you work with people who (1) understand how difficult it is to complete a project, (2) know it will probably take longer to complete a project when no one's getting paid, and (3) are not too ambitious. By "not too ambitious," I mean that no one is trying to make something that's beyond their skill sets.

Nonmod Projects

You can work on nonmod projects, but you should keep the same expectations in mind. Everyone you work with needs to understand how much more difficult it will be to develop a game when no one is getting paid, and they will have to find the time and energy to invest in it when they're not working their day jobs.

GET GIGS IN ADJACENT INDUSTRIES

Sometimes, I think people get the perspective that if they're trying to be a part of the game industry, they can't do *anything else*. If they take a job outside of games after trying to find an elusive game gig, they've somehow failed. For me, this is the wrong way to look at things. Any type of writing job—in any industry—is going to make you a better writer. The same is true for any editing job and your growth as an editor. In addition, that job outside of games still grows the skills you'll need for games, and it adds to your work history. This is impressive experience to have. Plus, it keeps you paid.

Get work where you can find it.

The oldest client I have is a university. I copyedit their online courses. I can definitely say that it's sharpened my editing skills. In the past few years, I've gotten both copyediting and developmental editing work on game projects. My work with this university client, for as long as I've been with them, has proved my expertise as an editor.

 INTERVIEW WITH LISA HUNTER

Lisa Hunter is a Narrative Director for Compulsion Games, an Xbox first-party studio. Before joining Compulsion in 2016, she was a screenwriter for film and television, with nearly 100 produced credits. She cocreated Cirque du Soleil's TV series Big Top Academy *and was head writer on the International Emmy-nominated kids' series* Look Kool. *She has a B.A. in writing from Barnard College.*

What led you to pursue freelancing, instead of employment?

When I lived in New York, I always had full-time jobs just to have health insurance. When I moved to Montreal (to be with my partner), I suddenly didn't need a full-time job to have that security net anymore because of Canada's social safety net. The freedom to become a freelancer was scary but also exciting.

Did you get your start in games, TV, or film? What led to a desire to work in the other two?

I started in television, but was simultaneously working on film projects, too. That's normal in Canada—people go back and forth here. In the States, you used to be categorized as one type of writer or the other (though that's changing now, too, with the ubiquity of streaming services). I like working in both TV and film, depending on whether I want to write a fictional world for multiple episodes, or whether I want to tell the single most important story in a character's life (which is what film tends to be). Games are a weird hybrid—for a big AAA game, you have reams of content like TV, but the overarching story is often a film-like hero's journey.

You could focus solely on one of these industries, or even only two of them. What motivates you to work in all three?

For a long time, I hesitated to work in games. The "ethics in games journalism" brouhaha happened just as I was on the cusp of moving into the industry. I hesitated for a couple of years because I was frankly afraid of what might happen. But I dipped a toe in as a contractor, and then the company offered me a full-time job, and it's been great. My studio is a safe and respectful place for women to work. These days, I only do small screenwriting gigs here and there, and only for projects I absolutely love. But I do find I'm able to squeeze them into my schedule. It's amazing how much more time I have to write now that I am not always looking for the next freelance job.

Is it easier to get gigs because you work in all three?

There's an advantage to having multiple skill sets, because you get three times the career options, plus you have the aura of seeming hard to get. :-)

If, say, you've got a gig in film, will you also look for work in TV and games at the same time, or do you prefer to focus on working in one industry at a time?

When I started as a contract writer for Compulsion, I only worked about 20 hours a week, so I was also doing film and TV at the same time. I found that I either needed to devote a whole day to just one thing, or I needed to take a nap or walk in between working on competing projects. I called it a "brain wipe." Juggling multiple projects requires being able to compartmentalize to be able to go between worlds. It's not easy! The Rule of Freelance is that you have either no work or three projects all with the same urgent deadline. These days, working on just one project feels like a luxury.

Have you developed skills or processes writing for TV and film that have benefited your work for games?

TV teaches you to write fast—a 30-page script in a week is standard turnaround. Like games, it's collaborative, with many moving parts. And because I'd been a head writer for TV, I also had some production skills (scheduling, estimating how long things will take, etc.). So for me, a TV background was a huge help. That said, our two most recent narrative hires got the nod because of their spectacular indie Twine games. So there's more than one kind of path to the same place.

And have you developed skills or processes writing for games that have benefited your work for TV and film?

Now that I work in games, I don't work nearly as much in other media, so there isn't a direct benefit to my game experience. But I could totally see that someone who started in games could use their skill set for TV—again, the collaborative nature of the teams, the thick skin needed for iteration, and so on. Whichever media you start in will be a benefit in the second one.

Have you ever gotten a game gig because of your work in film or TV? What did your client appreciate about your experience in those industries?

I absolutely got my game career because of my TV work. However, I went to a studio known for narrative games with cinematic-style cutscenes and stories. If I'd gone to a different kind of studio, the learning curve would have been much steeper. I've been taking narrative design classes to learn how other types of games tell stories without the traditional cutscene model. I find that really exciting and challenging, and am planning to make some small personal games, so I can tell stories in a different way.

What advice would you give to writers who have experience in other storytelling media and are looking to get into games? How can they use their history in and knowledge of those media to sell themselves to game clients?

Writers are starting to move more fluidly between games and screenwriting these days, or at least it seems that way in Montreal. What *doesn't* work is to give the impression that you're "slumming" in games just for a paycheck. I see that attitude from some screenwriters: "I don't play games, but that's where the work is. How do I break in? By pitching Ubisoft my game idea?" Ugh. Don't do this!

GAINING EXPERIENCE IS EASIER THAN YOU THINK

Hopefully, by the time you got to the end of this chapter, you felt much better about your level of experience. Maybe you had experience and you didn't know it, like a game jam project or a mod (whether you worked on that mod as a part of a team or on your own, it counts).

If you don't have a game yet, lean into your experience outside of games that makes you an expert in storytelling. Market yourself as someone who's knowledgeable about the fundamentals of great stories, while you take on small projects like designing Twine games that you can add to your portfolio.

EXERCISES

What Experience *Do* You Have?

Do a self-assessment of your storytelling experience in and outside of games, and make a list. Be sure to note

- your educational background,

- any writing work in adjacent industries,

- any publications you may have outside of games,

- any game jams you were a part of,

- any games you made with a tool like Twine or a mod.

Anything on this list is relevant experience that you can use to market yourself and your skills.

Find a Game Jam

Go to Itch.io, and review upcoming game jams. Which of these look interesting to you? Which of them would fit into your schedule?

If you're ready, join a game jam.

NOTES

1. "History of the Video Game Industry," Drexel University, accessed November 11, 2021, http://www.pages.drexel.edu/~as3445/history.html.
2. The critpath (or critical path) is all of the gameplay and narrative elements the player must complete to finish the game, as opposed to sidequests and optional branching narrative.
3. Conditions and variables are used to track players' specific choices throughout their game and give them specific events, missions/quests, NPC relationships, and dialogue options based on those choices.
4. David Gaider, "Do You Want to Write Video Games?," Polygon, August 15, 2016, https://www.polygon.com/2016/8/15/12455728/how-to-get-a-job-writing-games-maybe.
5. Megan Decleene, "The Forgotten City, Once an Award-Winning *Skyrim* Mod, Is Out as a Standalone Game Today," The Gamer, last modified July 28, 2021, https://www.thegamer.com/the-forgotten-city-skyrim-mod-standalone-game-out-today/.

CHAPTER 10

The Online (?) Portfolio

One of the questions I get in one-on-one conversations and on panels is "What do I need to put in my portfolio?" It's one of the most important questions you have to consider, whether you're looking to freelance or get employed work. There's a good reason why freelancers are so concerned about their portfolio, what to put in it, and whether it's good enough. The portfolio speaks on your behalf. It's the literal embodiment of your talents and your flexibility as a writer.

And, forgive me for riffing off this old cliché, but you can *tell* people what you can do; your portfolio *shows* it.

Let's explore what goes into a portfolio:

- What should you include? What shouldn't you include?

- How do you organize your portfolio website?

- How do you make your website accessible and easy to read?

- Do you need to maintain your presence on social media?

WHAT TO INCLUDE IN A WRITING PORTFOLIO

It's important to have a writing portfolio of work that represents who you are (or who you're trying to be) and what you've done in the industry. The

DOI: 10.1201/9781003199779-12

portfolio speaks on your behalf. While you can tell someone what you're capable of, your portfolio samples are *proof.*

Your writing portfolio has a couple of goals

- to illustrate your narrative skills and experience, and

- to show your technical writing and communication proficiency.

Writers are very aware that a portfolio needs to prove how good they are at storytelling, but being a good technical writer and communicator is equally as important. If you haven't thought about technical writing and formatting, now is a good time to review your samples for those characteristics.

> Missing some of the samples in your portfolio that I mention here? You can find templates for them at *The Game Narrative Toolbox's* companion website: https://routledgetextbooks.com/textbooks/9781138787087/. You can also review portfolios of other game writers and narrative designers to get a feel for certain types of documents and how you can format them.

Narrative Design and Game Writing Docs

As a narrative designer and game writer, you may be required to write all kinds of documents at any given time for any given project. The following are typical documents you might be responsible for producing, and it's a good idea to have these samples in your portfolio.

Worldbuilding Docs

Game/Story/Universe Bibles   This is usually what people think of when they hear "worldbuilding documentation." It's that large document with the big table of contents and multiple sections. Timelines, cultures and societies, and fighting and magic systems are all found in the bible. The bible is *the* encyclopedia about the world.

For Your Portfolio

You don't want to include an entire bible. These can be quite long. Even a shorter bible of 20 or so pages is a lot. Include excerpts. That might be a detailed timeline, the description of an important location, the summary of an important historical event, etc.

World Overview Document

This is the summary of the world and highlights aspects of it, including locations, characters, and cultures, and how they will feature in the game and the game's story. You can think of it as a "starter" document or a brief. The information in the overview document will be further developed, most likely in the bible, in concept art, and in game design docs.

For Your Portfolio

A sample world overview document can be around two to four pages. This is the perfect length for a portfolio piece.

Character Bios

Character bios tend to be a part of bibles, but you want these to stand on their own in your portfolio. Bios include everything the team needs to know about the characters. Physical descriptions, personalities, likes and dislikes, motivations, histories. You might even note the character's development throughout the game, character arcs, and any significant relationships with other characters.

For Your Portfolio

Bios can be quite detailed or a short paragraph, depending on the game and how story-oriented (or not) it is. They can also take on different tones and styles, reflecting the content of the game. You'll want to have several bios of different lengths for different genres. For example, a character bio for an interactive fiction game might be more detailed and explain the relationships the character can have with other characters, including love interests. Another bio might be for a clicker. It's written in a humorous tone, and there's one paragraph giving the character's history and motivations.

Lore and Flavor Text

Lore passages can be long or short, while flavor text should be short. Lore is what the player finds in the world in the form of books, journals, e-mails, scrolls, letters, etc., or in menus. Flavor text is short descriptors for locations, weapons, other items, etc. Lore and flavor text give players insight about the world beyond the gameplay.

For Your Portfolio

You have a lot of freedom in what you write for these and how you format them for your portfolio. For lore, you can include poems, text messages, fables, notes left on scraps of paper, etc. For flavor text, you can write descriptions for any kind of object you can think of. Show off your versatility as a writer when it comes to tones and styles. If you're good at humor, don't forget to have humorous samples!

Story Document

Story documents are more appropriate for shorter games, games that aren't story oriented, or for when you need to outline the story in a separate document. It's good to feature a story synopsis, main plot points, and plot summaries per level, mission, or quest.

For Your Portfolio

While story documents might be for shorter documents, they can be more than ten pages. Like the bible, use excerpts of a story document. Show off different kinds of content and different formatting techniques for that content.

Quests/Missions

Show the progression of the quest or mission in your documentation. Include (1) the informational text that guides the player, (2) clearly defined objectives for each part of the quest, (3) characters involved, (4) choices the player will decide between, and (5) dialogue from quest givers. As is typical of all documentation in the industry, there's no standard format for quests and missions. Structure and organize your quests in a way that's easy to follow and makes sense for how they progress.

For Your Portfolio

A short quest chain (maybe three or four quests) illustrates how you plot quests and missions, how you develop the player-character and NPCs over the duration of the quest/mission, and how you bring the quest/mission to a satisfying end.

Cutscenes/Cinematic Scripts

Cutscenes and cinematics are what people (including a lot of devs) think of as "story" when it comes to games. Some players appreciate them. Others just press the skip button as soon as the cutscene or cinematic starts.

Cutscenes and cinematics are typically written in screenplay format. However, if the cutscene is an animatic or in the style of comic book panels appearing in sequence, comic script formatting might make more sense.

For Your Portfolio

Have some cutscenes and cinematics of different lengths and for stories in different settings, keeping in mind that a long scene is only around 2–3 minutes. You certainly don't want your samples to be *Metal Gear*-like in length (you ain't Kojima). Be sure to note where the gameplay resumes or if there's a gameplay sequence between parts of the scene.

Barks

Writing barks seems to be a "love it" or "hate it" task among the writers I know. Writing 100 different ways to say "Grenade!" or "Incoming!" or coming up with enough variations of "Hello," so the player doesn't tire of hearing the lines is akin to torture for some writers. For others, they love writing barks. It's a fun challenge. And, since so many writers want to avoid writing barks, writers who are willing to draft barks have less competition.

For Your Portfolio

However you format your barks document, make it clear what the original line is. For example, you might label the top cell of a spreadsheet column "100 ways to say 'Look out!'." Spreadsheets, by the way, are great for barks writing.[1]

Game Design Documents

You might find yourself responsible for writing a game design document (GDD) as the narrative designer or game writer on the project. Writing GDDs is also a service you can offer to developers.

For Your Portfolio

Strong technical writing skills, while important for any game doc you write, are essential in drafting and organizing a GDD. Make sure your content flows well and is easy to digest. Have a couple of types of game genres represented.

GDDs can be quite long. Ten pages from a section might be too long, but you have a couple of excerpts that illustrate the kind of information you would find in a GDD, like a gameplay summary, mapping out levels, and character classes.

A General Note about Samples

As I mentioned with character bios, it's important to keep in mind that the less story-oriented the game is, the less detailed the information in your documents is going to be, and vice versa. Why is this a big deal? You want to prove that you can produce what's appropriate for the game. A common horror story devs will tell about working with writers is the walls and walls and walls of text the writers will turn in, not understanding the text box can only fit 200 characters comfortably. An RPG will need more detailed content in its documentation, and a match-3 will need less detailed content. Your portfolio pieces should illustrate that you understand the differences between genres.

Game Genres, Settings, and Tones

Make sure you have story samples for different game genres, settings, and tones. The more variety you have, the less you'll have to worry about quickly writing a sample when you want to apply for a particular job, and you don't have *any* pieces that will fit the project in question. It's particularly frustrating when you see a job that's your ideal fit, or a prospective client reviews your online portfolio, and you don't have the right pieces to show them.

Here are lists of the types of genres, settings, and tones you can include in your portfolio (these are by no means exhaustive). If you don't want to write for a particular genre or setting, don't feel forced to add it.

Game Genres

- Action-adventure
- Casual mobile
  - Match-3, clicker, decorating, etc.
- Hidden object
- Interactive fiction
  - Visual novels, text-based games
- Kid's games
- Life simulation
- Platformers
- RPGs
  - First person, third person

- Shooters
  - First person, third person
- Simulations
- Sports

Settings

- Medieval fantasy
- Near-future science fiction
- Real world
- Space opera
- Dystopia
- Urban fantasy
- Cyberpunk

Tones

- Absurd/Bizarre
- Horror
- Humorous
- Noir
- Parodic
- Romantic
- Satirical

 INTERVIEW WITH ANNA MEGILL

Anna Megill is an award-winning game writer and industry veteran with experience writing primarily for modern AAA games. In her 17 years of game development, Anna has worked for some of the top studios around the world, such as Ubisoft, Arkane, Square Enix, Remedy, and Nintendo. Anna has written dozens of published video games in her career, including

two Games of the Year. She also provides resources and advice to aspiring writers through her website and through an upcoming guidebook for game writers. Anna currently works at Playground Games on their upcoming Fable *game.*

What led you to pursue freelancing, instead of employment?

Honestly? Exhaustion. I needed a break from the intense focus of AAA dev life. Freelancing let me choose my own projects and set my own schedule. Don't get me wrong—I love the deep dive into game story that you get when you clock in day after day to a big AAA project for several years. But it can be a high-pressure environment. I wanted to work on my own time and in my own way for a while.

There's a fascinating reason why you no longer have an online portfolio. Can you tell that story?

I'd given some samples to the IGDA Writing SIG as examples of how to write an RPG quest—just a few excerpts from *Guild Wars 2*. They were posted online for a while without incident, and years passed. I became a hiring manager at a major studio and was reviewing samples for a writing role, when I came across a sample that seemed familiar. I squinted at it for a moment, trying to decide where I knew it from. And then it hit me: It was my quest! My writing. Someone had taken one of my *GW2* quests and slightly reworded it, so it wasn't obvious plagiarism, then submitted it as their own writing sample. They'd done a good job because I didn't immediately recognize my own work. But the concepts, the structure, even most of the wording, were too similar to fool me for long. I don't know how long they'd been passing it off as their own work, but I wrote them a scathing e-mail telling them to stop. Then I pulled my samples from the IGDA site. Now, I still have an online portfolio, but everything is hidden and password protected. Lesson learned.

You've reviewed portfolios when hiring writers. Have people sent other samples they plagiarized? How did you know they were plagiarized?

I rarely see plagiarism, but it does happen. There are two kinds: Someone trying to mimic writing from a critically acclaimed game and not changing it enough to make it their own. And the far rarer case where someone explicitly takes a published screenplay and submits it as their own. The first type is a sincere mistake. The second type is more sinister. But either way, you're probably not getting the job if I recognize your sample as someone else's work. And I usually do, because I play most games out there. Or at least see enough to get a sense of the style and voice of the IP.

There's an expectation that people will link to their online portfolios in queries or cover letters. What do you say to prospective clients and employers in your e-mails to explain that your portfolio isn't online?

Well, my portfolio is online, just well-hidden and protected. But I do sometimes submit a .pdf of my work instead of linking to it online. And I've had candidates do that for me as a hiring manager. It's fine, honestly. I think that's normal enough that it doesn't require much explanation. As long as I can see some samples, we're good.

What has been your strategy for choosing the right portfolio pieces to send when you're applying for work, especially when the listing isn't clear about the type of samples you should send?

I look at the studio's work to see if there's a house style or tone I can match. For example, if I were applying to Naughty Dog and there was no indication of what IP the role was for, I'd still know what to submit. Even though there's a huge tonal difference between *Uncharted* and *The Last of Us*, I know that they want highly cinematic writing, with well-developed, realistic characters, in a generally real-world setting. That helps narrow down my options. Then I choose my strongest writing to fit those requirements and provide a range of narrative work: cinematics, barks, conversations. Sometimes I whip up bespoke pieces for an application if I don't have anything appropriate. Maybe a mission containing the full range of narrative possibilities. But that's not something I recommend. It's better to go with published work or with samples you've thoroughly vetted.

Beyond the specifics in application guidelines, what do you like to see in a writer's portfolio samples?

The sample parameters and tone aside, what I'm looking for is an understanding of interactive writing. Do you understand how game writing differs from other kinds of writing? How do you handle the unique requirements of maneuvering players around a scene and getting the critical information while keeping them entertained? Your samples should show me that. If all you've got is a list of barks, that's okay. Give me some context to understand when and where those fire in the game and how they impact the story. A good bark can do a lot of narrative work. Show me that you understand that.

Is there anything you're tired of seeing in writing samples? Maybe a weakness that writers don't realize is hurting the overall impression of their work?

What I'm most tired of is Generic Game Text. This is a problem for newer writers, especially as they don't have a lot of published work and are trying to fill out their portfolio with samples. They tend to write pieces for a hypothetical Every Game. It's usually a shooter or fantasy RPG, but not a *specific* one. So all the lines feel generic and clichéd. Great that you know how to write a dozen versions of "Need some ammo" or "Buy my potion," but you're not telling me anything about your voice as a writer. I'd rather see creative, original lines that represent your take on an existing game or come from some game you dreamed up than see flawless-but-trite general lines.

If you could recommend a couple of things writers and narrative designers could do to improve their portfolios, what would those be?

Candidates should let other writers see their work and give feedback. It's critical to have an objective set of eyes review your portfolio holistically and see how you're coming across. You may be great at gritty, noir pieces, but it says something about you as a writer if that's the only thing in your portfolio. Try to show range with your samples. It's okay to specialize or have a signature style, but include enough other work, so I know you can write in whatever style the project requires. And tell me who you are with your portfolio. Your work should show growth or at least progression. If you're writing the same stuff you wrote ten years ago, what have you done with that time? What have you learned? Above all, make it easy to read. The more hoops I have to jump through to read a screenplay, the less likely I am to see it. I had one candidate send us links to her Patreon page. Her samples were locked behind a monthly donation paywall. I respect her hustle, but sorry. There's no way I'm paying to view someone's writing sample. Make it easy for me to see what a great writer you are.

In your opinion, what does a strong writing portfolio include?

My ideal portfolio would have a wide range of samples that tell me who the applicant is as a writer. It would showcase a variety of styles and tones. And there'd be video of the work in game to accompany the screenplays and other samples. All of it would be easily reached by clicking a link. Yeah. That's the dream.

Technical Writing and Communication

Strong Technical Writing

The second goal of your samples is to illustrate that you have sound technical writing skills and can communicate effectively through technical documentation.

Documents are always written *for* audiences, and there are audience expectations because of this. You don't want to discount audience expectations. It's like having expectations for game genres. If you're playing a platformer, you're going to expect some jumping mechanics. If you're reading a character bio, you're going to want to understand that character's personality.

So, narrative design and game writing docs fall under the category of technical writing. Therefore, your audience is going to expect that you follow the tenets of good technical writing. Prospective clients will be reviewing your samples not only as storytelling documents, but also as technical ones. I am not saying that every time they read a document, they will be actively thinking, "Is this a well-written technical doc?" However, they will respond to how your document is formatted, whether or not it is easy to read, and whether or not it is accessible to everyone on the team.

Technical documentation has the following characteristics:

- Highly structured and organized

- Clearly and concisely communicated

- Easy to understand

- Clearly and concisely explained

The purpose of technical writing (generally speaking) is to give the reader a better understanding of a certain subject or topic.

For example, the purpose of a worldbuilding doc is to give the team explanations about the world and how it works, its role in the game, and its presentation/interaction with players.

When your team is the audience, there are a few things to keep in mind:

Each team member approaches reading differently. That means they have different reading strengths and weaknesses. That means some of them don't like reading *at all*. Be honest for a second: Do you like reading? I'll be honest—I don't always like to read. Sometimes, when I open an e-mail or a document on my phone, if I see a wall of text and I can't figure out in a half second what I'm supposed to get out of it, I put it aside for later, especially if I'm tired or busy. I don't have the bandwidth for it.

Each team member will digest what they've read differently. Reading comprehension skills vary. The types of things they read will affect how they approach the text in the document.

The writing in the document should be accessible to the *entire* audience.

And when you're making the document accessible, keep in mind what each discipline needs to know and what they care about. Animators may not care about a character's backstory. However, the character's personality and demeanor may inform how the character moves. Does the character walk hunched over? Is it a nervous creature that skitters across walls? Those movements are going to have to be animated, so the only information in the character bio that applies directly to the animator may be the character's demeanor and personality.

If you're writing new samples for your portfolio, have an imaginary team of developers in mind. They're your audience. You're preparing this document for game designers, artists, animators, programmers, UI designers, musicians, sound engineers, etc.

For any of your existing samples, you may want to do a technical formatting pass. Can you make the document easier to read? Can you break up text with bullet points or white space? Can you rearrange the content, so the information nonwriters need is toward the beginning of the document, and they don't have to dig through pages to find what's relevant to their work?

Keep in Mind While Formatting… Not everyone likes to read. → Most developers I've worked with do not.

In any section or subsection, put first information for nonwriters and team members who won't be making major decisions about the direction of the story or game (programmers, level designers, sound designers, artists, animators, etc.).

As I mentioned earlier, not everyone likes to read. Most of the developers I've worked with don't like reading, and *I* don't always like reading when I have to work my way through a big block of text. I want to be able to quickly look at something and figure out what I need to take away from it. Assume that a prospective client, when first reviewing your application, will be skimming your samples. Make it easy for them to pick out the important bits. If you pass that first review, they'll likely read your work more thoroughly.

For example, you want to put descriptions at the beginning of sections because they can be read quickly, and you won't force people to "fish" for that information. These are your quick "stats." For a location, these could be the city or region where the location is, any fictional or real-life analogues that will help people get a better picture of the location, the functional uses of that location (why do people gather there, why is it important), and so on.

FORMATTING TECHNIQUES

- Use bullet points whenever you can. (If you don't have to use paragraphs, don't.)
- Use short sentences or phrases whenever you can.
- Use white space, phrases, and bullet points to draw the eye. If you look at the two examples (the bulleted text and the wall of text), look at what draws your eye.

  Sound effects should also accompany player-character and NPC actions. This will make the game more immersive and interesting. Possible sound effects: object interaction in the game world and loot, impact of weapons (melee weapons, ranged weapons, and firearms all have their own sounds), police car sirens and tank blasts.

  Sound Effects should also accompany player-character and NPC actions. This will make the game more immersive and interesting. Possible sound effects:

  - Object interaction in the game world and loot
  - Impact of weapons (melee weapons, ranged weapons, and firearms all have their own sounds)
  - Police car sirens and tank blasts

  It's difficult to know where to look with the block of text. But with white text and bullet points, you can see the list. You can see what's highlighted. You can see what's called out. Both examples, by the way, are the exact same words, only formatted differently.
- Put paragraphs at the end of the section or subsection (for example, narrating a character's history). Paragraphs are going to contain a lot more detail. They tend to be lore heavy. The members of the team who are going to need to know this are other narrative designers and writers who are going to be fleshing out the story, game designers who need to understand the narrative design and how it's integrated into the gameplay, and the producers and directors who need to understand the game's content.

At the same time, keep your paragraphs readable. You want them to be shorter and not longer.

Most people are reading on screens these days. Reading long paragraphs on screens is difficult on the eyes. *Always* make things easier on those who are looking to hire you!

BUT MY WORK'S UNDER NDA!

At least one client recognized your talent, you worked on the game(s), and now you can't show it to anyone because that work is under NDA.

This isn't the roadblock that it might seem to be. You can always *ask* a client if you can put work still under NDA in your portfolio. Sure, they can always say no, especially if the game hasn't been released, but it also benefits them to allow you to show off your work. It shows another developer the quality of writing* in their game. If you think a client might be hesitant because the writing in question is from a game that hasn't yet been released, you can tell your client you won't include the samples in a public portfolio.

For the record, I've asked a couple of my clients if I could add work under NDA to my portfolio. None of them have said no.

*If you're not a writer, you can still use this strategy.

Completing the Portfolio

You may not have existing samples you can put in your portfolio, either because they're under NDA, or you haven't worked on a project that required you to develop the documentation. If this is your situation, you can still write samples that fill those gaps. In the early days of my portfolio, I had to create samples in areas I was lacking. I made up a couple of quick game scenarios for cutscenes and character bios. These scenarios were not complicated by any means. They were just to give me an idea for a scene and for a couple of characters who might appear in the game.

Set aside a few hours a week to write your new portfolio pieces. When you're working on these samples, take note of how long it takes you to produce each one. This will give you a sense of how time consuming they are. The more you write these kinds of documents, the more efficient you'll get, and the less time it will take.

When you feel good about your draft, have at least one person critique it for you. This can be another writer or narrative designer, but you might also reach out to a dev who's not a writer but understands narrative design. Get feedback on the following:

- Is your writing clear? Is anything confusing, and why?

- Is it a successful sample for its documentation type? (For example, it reads like a cinematic and is properly formatted as a cinematic.)

- Is your vision for the narrative clear?

- Is it easy to read and understand from a narrative perspective?

- Is it a sound technical document?

- How could you improve the formatting from a technical aspect?

Make sure you give your reviewer(s) some kind of comparable payment, even if it's just trading services or giving them feedback on one of their projects.

PLAY YOUR PORTFOLIO

It's one thing for someone to see your writing on a page or screen. It's another to see it in action and watch players interact with it. Footage of your in-game writing literally brings your work to life and demonstrates how the player experiences your writing and design.

Find let's plays, walkthroughs, or streams for your games on Twitch and YouTube. If you can't find samples from content creators, consider playing parts of the game yourself.[2] You don't have to narrate—just provide video with your work.

Sometimes, you may have to get creative, especially if you have samples for text-based games. I found a forum for *Academagia*, the first game I worked on with Black Chicken Studios. One of the players copied and pasted a DLC I had written, along with their choices and their thought processes for making certain choices. I took screenshots of this let's play and put them into a PDF.

WATERMARK YOUR SAMPLES!

As I discovered while teaching at ITT, and as Anna Megill can attest to, plagiarism is a huge problem. People even copy and paste LinkedIn profiles. One way to protect your work against plagiarism is to watermark everything and save your documents as PDF files. You can watermark with your logo if you have one or use text.

Watermarking isn't a failsafe against plagiarists. However, watermarks are difficult to remove. If plagiarists are too lazy to do their own work, they probably won't want to put in the effort to remove your watermarks.

YOUR ONLINE PRESENCE

Having an online portfolio with clearly marked samples is a must. It's not only a way for people you've talked to to look up your work online, but it's also a way for people to *find* you. People contact me occasionally when they find me through my website, and I have not reached out to them first. I've gotten several jobs this way.

The types of clients and employers you want to attract are going to vet you, so give them a good impression with your website and your online portfolio.

Your website doesn't need to be sexy[3]—it needs to be readable. There are several website builders like Wix, Site123, and WordPress. (The one disadvantage to free accounts is that the name of the company will appear in your domain name.) Website builders offer clean, organized templates you can plug your work into. They also allow you to customize these templates by changing colors, fonts, etc., or let you come up with your own design. You can do a search for website builders to see which will work best for you.

Before You Publish Your Website

Make sure your writing is error free. Proofread, proofread again, and proofread some more. Have others proofread it. Not everyone can identify typos and grammatical errors, but you don't want to take that chance. People *will* notice clunky, awkward writing.

Easy Access Is Key

Include everything you do in your portfolio. If you also write prose, scripts for TV or film, or comics, have separate pages on your website with those samples. I do have prose featured with different genres noted. If game developers, or comics publishers, etc., visit my site, they can see that I work in different genres and get a sense of my range. Clients appreciate your flexibility and experience in other media.

I did look at several portfolios before I designed mine. One thing I noticed is that some writers have similar media together, like film and games. It might be difficult for people to find the samples they want to look at, even if you label them clearly. Keep in mind that sometimes people don't read carefully. If you do work in several media, make sure that you do not mix up your samples. Don't include comic scripts and game writing on the same page. As a prospective client, I don't want to go to that page and try to find your narrative design samples amidst your comics writing. Vetting freelancers is time consuming. And having a page that's confusing or that makes it difficult for someone to find what they're looking for can waste their time. If it's too difficult or confusing to find the relevant samples, they may leave your website all together and move on to someone else. Remember, don't make it easy to reject you.

Do clearly label each of your samples. Note that it's an excerpt from a bible or a detailed character bio. Say that it's lore from a science fiction RPG, etc. Categorizing your samples like this makes it easier for visitors to find what they're looking for and, at a glance, they can see that you have experience working in certain roles, genres, and style.

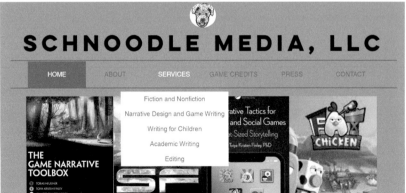

My homepage and the drop-down menu for the different pages on my website.

The Contact Form

Always have a way for a prospective client to get in touch with you! Some freelancers don't include an e-mail address or contact form on their websites. There *might* be social media links, but DMs aren't great for longer communications. I've listened to friends vent about writers they wanted to contact to find out their availability or include them on a project, only to discover the writers' websites offered no way to get in touch with them.

There are good reasons why you might not want your contact information publicly online. Stalking and harassment are very real threats, especially for those in marginalized groups. Website builders have templates for contact forms. You don't have to reveal your e-mail address, and you can choose what information you want the person contacting you to reveal. Their message goes to the inbox of your choice. You can then choose to respond to them from that e-mail address, or you can respond from your website provider's site, keeping your e-mail address hidden.

When you're researching potential website providers, see if they have templates for contact forms and if they keep your e-mail address private.

ORGANIZING YOUR PORTFOLIO

The Pages You'll Need

Your website is part of your marketing, as it literally markets your abilities and experiences. While you can design (or have someone design for you) it in any number of ways, there are pages and content that are prerequisites for a portfolio that is an accurate representation of your business and is easy to navigate.

Homepage

This is your website's "opening." It's the eye-catching introduction that makes visitors want to peruse your website's other pages and get to your actual portfolio. Don't add too many images on your homepage. For functional reasons, it can cause the site to load more slowly. Most users won't wait more than 15 seconds.[4] A few images representing your work, in and out of games, is a good way to greet visitors.

Other essential information for the homepage:

- Your name and/or the name of your freelancing business.

- A summary or list of your services.

- Contact information.

- Social media presences (templates provide Twitter, Facebook, LinkedIn, etc., icons, and you can link to them).

THE HEADER WITH NAVIGATION MENU OR NAVIGATION BAR

Just like it sounds, the header with navigation menu or bar appears at the top of the page. For blog-like interfaces, it may appear on the left- or right-hand side of the screen with the pages listed in a column.

Your site's public pages will appear here. Think carefully about what you name your pages. A visitor should be able to read them and immediately know what kind of content they can find on those pages. For example, if you've worked in both games and TV, you can name one page "Game Writing" and the other "TV Scripts."

Website builders have templates with headers and menus. You can customize where these are located on your pages, the font, and the font color.

DROP-DOWN MENUS AND SUBPAGES

Sometimes, you might have a lot of pages on your website. I have narrative design and game writing, prose fiction and nonfiction, children's writing, academic writing, and editing pages. If I listed all of those pages in my header, it would be pretty crowded. A quick fix is grouping them into subpages.

I grouped all of these pages into "Services." When a visitor hovers over "Services," a drop-down menu lists all of those pages.

Think about how you can group your pages into subpages to keep your website tidy.

About Page

This is where you can add longer, more detailed information about you, your work and experience, and your freelance services. You might also consider adding your business philosophy, your vision for working with clients, and anything that will give visitors a better sense of who you are and how you run your business.

Portfolio Pages

Here's where you link to your samples. Each of these pages houses your portfolio pieces. Don't mix up your samples. In other words, if you're a novelist and a game writer, don't arrange your game writing samples in a way that the visitor can't tell the difference between what's prose fiction and what's game samples. If you have quite a few samples for more than one medium, create separate pages for each medium in which you work. If your samples for both aren't enough for separate pages, you can split up the page—but make it clear to the visitor what's what.

Game Credits

Having your game credits in your portfolio is a must. Credits tell the prospective client that you have been involved in game development and have experience. You can give your credits their own page or list them with your game samples. Make sure you include *all* projects you've worked on, even if they're your personal projects. For example, jam games, class projects, and your own Twine games are legitimate games, and you should list them.

I even note unreleased projects on my credits page. Working on projects that never get released is an industry standard (and a right of passage). Prospective clients will be sympathetic to this, and they've probably been a part of unreleased projects themselves.

Great Pages/Content to Add

You can have the following dedicated pages on your site, or you might incorporate them in existing pages via text or hyperlink.

Press/News/Testimonials

This information is evidence that your work has been well received. Press or news coverage could be on any of your panels, talks, or lectures. This shows that your ideas are out in the public, and they're valued. You can also add any coverage or reviews of games you worked on.

Praise from your clients in the form of testimonials are also important for your site. During their vetting process, prospective clients will see from testimonials that you've provided great work to clients in the past, and you can do the same for them. If you don't have testimonials from clients, feel free to reach out to them. They may have expressed in an e-mail or another communication how pleased they were with your work or how you made an impact on their project. Simply ask for permission if you can quote them on your website.

WHO CAN TESTIFY?

Do you have clients you can reach out to and ask them for testimonials?

Make a quick list of these clients, and ask them.

Also, look through e-mails, DMs, etc., and see if any praise they've given you would make a good quote. (When a client does praise you, it is hard to forget!)

CV/Résumé

You can give your CV or résumé its own page or link to it from your about page, homepage, or wherever you have your bio. Some prospective clients really care about seeing your CV/résumé, while applications, interviews, samples, and referrals will carry much more weight with others.

Blog

If you have a blog that's relevant to your work, you might link to it on your portfolio website. Your blog posts will be enlightening to a prospective client if they get a view into your philosophy about your work or games in general. Whether you analyze games, review stories in other media like TV or film, or talk about pop culture in general, this can clue the client in to how you think about media and narrative, and it gives them a sense of your voice.

Don't feel as if you *have* to have a blog to attract clients. (To be honest, I find it difficult to keep any kind of consistent schedule to produce content for a blog.) It's something to include if you already have it.

THE PRIVATE PORTFOLIO

You don't want to put all of your samples on your public portfolio, especially if you have a lot of them. For one, you don't want to force someone to wade through lots of links when they only need to see two or three. Remember, your public, online portfolio is more of an introduction. It's a taste of what you can do.

Have a reserve of samples for when you need to tailor the samples to specific applications and queries. For example, if you're applying to a narrative design gig for a mobile game, you would send quests you wrote for a mobile game that has a similar tone. You may have written 50 quests for that game, and you wouldn't want to put all 50 on your website (and you would likely need permission to use any of them as samples). However, two or three of the samples from a quest line would demonstrate to the prospective client how you structure quest plots and integrate them into the gameplay, how you develop the story through these plots, how you write NPC dialogue, and how you write instructional texts to guide the player through the quests.

Organize your private samples in a way that makes them easy to find and access when you're ready to send them to the prospective client. How you organize them, and where you organize them, is up to you—as long as you can quickly access them when you need them. It's time consuming when you know you have the perfect sample to illustrate what the client's looking for, and then you can't find it on your hard drive (definitely been there).

Also, if you're concerned about your work being plagiarized, you can store your samples on Drive (or another cloud service) and share their URLs with prospective clients, or you can password protect pages housing your samples and give out the passwords to prospective clients.

REMEMBER TO ASK YOURSELF: IS MY CONTENT ACCESSIBLE?

Make it easy for people to find what they need and to read your work. I've reviewed a few game developers' websites. The one major issue I have with them is that they're not well organized. I don't mean that they don't have relevant or good samples—I mean that I find it difficult to find what I need to know.

What I sometimes see, as I mentioned above, is a "mix" of samples. Game samples are mixed in with samples from other media. I don't know whether something is a game sample until I click on the link. I might end up clicking on several comics samples or a short story before I finally find something relevant to games. This can be frustrating for prospective clients searching for potential writers/narrative designers, or clients who are trying to vet candidates. It takes time they may not have, and they may simply move on from considering you.

It's also a good idea to label your game samples. Note what's a bible excerpt, a cinematic, a character bio, etc. So, for the bible excerpt, you might say "Bible Excerpt (Fantasy RPG)." This way, visitors can glance at links or captions and know exactly what they're about to review. Clearly labeled samples can also shorten their vetting process and answer questions about your experience with the genre, story setting, or tone of their game. You can label and categorize your nongame pieces this way, too.

EXERCISES

Gaps in Your Portfolio?

What types of game writing and narrative design docs are missing from your portfolio?

What styles and story genres are missing that you would be interested in writing?

Make a plan to write some samples. Over the next week, when would you have time to start drafting your first one?

Technical Writing Review

Choose a sample from your portfolio. Give it a technical writing pass.

How can you reformat and restructure the content so that it's easier to read and more accessible?

Anything under NDA?

Have you worked on games that have been released, or have you worked on projects that are still under NDA?

If the answer is yes,

1. make a list of these projects,

2. note your work from these projects you think would make good samples, and

3. write a practice e-mail asking the client for permission to use these samples.

Now, you have a letter! It's up to you whether you want to send it. It might feel a little strange to reach out and ask to use something that's still under NDA, but the worst the client can do is say no. (And nothing will have changed—you weren't using those samples anyway.)

NOTES

1. Some writers and narrative designers would say that spreadsheets are great for *all* writing documentation, since that's where so much of the writing ends up. I do not count myself in that group.
2. If you're not sure how to record and capture video, you can do a quick search for tutorial videos for Mac, PC, and Linux.
3. Unless you're a website/graphic designer.
4. "7 Essential Pages for Your Small Business Website," Freshonline.net, accessed November 11, 2021, https://freshonline.net/web-design/7-essential-pages-for-your-website/.

CHAPTER 11

Where to Find Work

Before we get into the meat of this chapter, I need to establish some expectations. I've moderated roundtables for new writers and co-moderated roundtables for freelancers, both at the Game Developers Conference. Sometimes, I'll get negative feedback because no one leading these discussions said plainly, "This is where you find work."

New freelancers—understandably—want to be told exactly where they need to go to find a gig. But this is a difficult thing to ask. Even if I could say to you right now, "Hey, I know of this job opening. You should go apply," there are going to be variables involved with the job that might make you a not-ideal candidate.

There is no magic answer to where you can find a gig.

There is no one place to go find work.

With that in mind, this chapter will give you advice on a number of things you can do to put yourself in the best position to get consistent work.

NETWORKING

The word "networking" can bring to mind schmoozing at fancy parties in business suits. A transactional exercise, complete strangers walk up to each other and list the highlights on their résumés or CVs. Once they get

DOI: 10.1201/9781003199779-13

deeper into the conversation, they discover whether the person they're talking to will be useful in helping them achieve their professional goals. As they walk away from each other, they make notes on the business card (if the person is useful) or lose the person's card (if not useful).

But networking is the lifeblood of any freelancer's business. You need your network—your community—to help you find work.

I don't want to sound as if you're simply using people to find a job and make money. Networking should be beneficial to everyone in your network. (For more on this, please see Chapter 3, "Your Network: It's More than the Contacts You Collect—It's Your Community.")

Join and Create Networking Channels

There are lots of places online where freelancers and others in the industry share job posts, ask for advice on a number of topics, and talk about their craft. Organizations like the International Game Developers Association (IGDA) have Facebook groups, Discord servers, and mailing lists. Devs have set up their own spaces for friends and acquaintances on social media platforms. If you're not sure where to find these groups, ask your friends and members in your network. Sometimes, you will need to answer questions to establish you're a part of the industry or that you'll be a good addition to the community,[1] or you'll need a referral.

Consider starting your own online communities, too. Invite people you know who would support each other and new members you might bring in. You don't want your sole focus to be on finding gigs, but that can be an important draw.

 INTERVIEW WITH HEIDI MCDONALD

Heidi McDonald is an award-winning narrative designer with over a decade of experience with direct and freelance game writing employment. Her special focuses include romance, science fiction, and empathy in games. When not writing or otherwise creating, she is staring thoughtfully at the moon shining over a cornfield somewhere in North Carolina—a place where it is perpetually Halloween.

What led you to pursue freelancing, instead of employment?
Necessity. I lost my job and faced difficulty finding another permanent hire position, mostly because I need remote work and I'm unable to relocate.

My partner and I care for a disabled elderly relative here at home, who can't be moved.

I found that in game writing, contract positions are much more numerous, and they tend to be much more supportive of remote work. I was hoping that the pandemic would mean more companies support remote work. It did for a while, yet I'm still seeing a majority of companies who expect relocation, and that's maddening. I hope we can arrive at a place in our industry where it's widely recognized that "writers rooms" CAN happen effectively, virtually, and that writing is one job that's not necessary to be onsite. The proof of this is that there were games still being released in 2020 and 2021.

One thing I don't think a lot of freelancers consider is reaching out to their networks and letting them know they're looking for work. Why do you think that is?

I think there are real stigmas around being unemployed, and around depending on your friends for help.

My dad and stepmother are Tupperware distributors. They always tried to get me to sell Tupperware. I felt very uneasy about the idea of doing that, not just because Tupperware is overpriced and bad for the environment, but also because succeeding at it involves capitalizing on people's friendships and guilt. Like, party guests will be pressured to buy expensive stuff they don't need, in order to get the host friend something they want for free. The salesperson is depending on that guest feeling like "I want to help my friend, and if I don't buy something, my friend won't get what she wants." I always found that to be really icky, and I had to go through some changes and reframing in my own mind before realizing that this looking-for-freelance-work thing is an entirely different situation than selling Tupperware. If people feel uncomfortable giving referrals, they won't, and that's okay. The number of folks who ARE okay with it will improve your prospects.

I will admit that one thing I have worried about is getting a reputation as "someone who's always looking for work." But the alternative is maybe not being able to make rent. This is literally about your survival. Working freelance is only partially about doing the actual contract work—you have to also be constantly hustling to set up more work, even as you work now. It's like that one scene in *Wallace and Gromit* where the dog is riding on top of a model train and literally simultaneously laying track down in front of him so that the train won't derail.

About unemployment: It sucks to lose your job. Most people who have been around the games industry for any length of time are used to getting let go for reasons outside of their control. In 2020, I lost half my contracts for reasons including studio closure, studio acquisition, pandemic caused a game cancellation, pandemic caused a budget change, and a company shifting to no longer hiring contractors. It's not necessarily you; it's the nature of our industry (and it's easy to lose sight of this in a capitalist society where "what you do" is often viewed as more important than "who you are," and productivity matters more than anything else).

Being unemployed can feel like an identity loss, or like there's something wrong with you, or like people will think you are incapable or lazy if you don't have a job. Most developers, though, are very familiar with this type of turbulence, have experienced it themselves, and are happy to retweet something to help a stranger in the industry that this has happened to.

The way to appeal to others without feeling guilty about it:

- Remember that they themselves have more than likely been unemployed at some point and because they know it's hard. They'll be willing to help.
- Realize that your friends care about you and want to see you succeed.
- Understand that you are responsible for your survival, and looking for work is about your survival.
- Make it a regular practice of giving referrals to others, without hesitation, even and especially at times when you are not looking for work. The street runs both ways. Other people are pleased to return the favor when you're the one in need, if you've gone out of your way to help them. I've tried to do that as much as I can.

One other point: When you ask people for leads, you're not asking for a charity handout, you're asking them to open a door. It's still going to be up to you to earn your way through that door, and to perform once you're through it. You're not asking for a handout. You're asking for a HAND UP, a boost that you can run with, and prove yourself worthy of.

When did it dawn on you that you could say to your friends and members of your network, "Hey, let me know if you see any jobs that would be good for me"?

It actually struck me as an immediate and logical first step. I can pore over opportunities just myself, or I can announce that I'm looking and have tons of sets of eyes all out looking at the same time. Finding work is a numbers game, so increasing your numbers increases your odds. You might find 25 leads on your own, and one or two of those turns into a couple of months of paying work. Increasing the number of leads you get coming in can only increase the amount of paying work that results in. Like because you have your 500 followers all keeping an eye out, now instead of 25 leads you get 50. It's just math.

You also never know which of your friends works somewhere that's about to hire more folks, which of them is hiring themselves, which of them has heard of opportunities that haven't hit LinkedIn or Indeed yet, or which of them has another friend for whom any of the foregoing is true. My current permanent hire job came from an unexpected referral. So, you really never know. But what CAN be quantified is the numbers. You can only increase your odds of success by casting a wider net.

Was it difficult to reach out to your network at first? What caused that hesitation?

After I lost my job in 2018, the shame was pretty huge. I was really visible in that position. And as both parties had signed mutual NDAs restricting anyone's ability to explain what happened, I didn't want people to think I was some kind of screw-up who employers shouldn't hire. It took me about a week to get okay with announcing that I was looking for work. I didn't want people asking questions or making unfavorable assumptions. I was super upset and feeling destabilized, and didn't want my bad news to scare or upset anyone.

Because, honestly, there are people for whom, if you admit vulnerability to them (like confessing that you're struggling with mental health or have had something unfortunate happen), they tune you out, they walk away, they say well-intentioned insensitive things, or they just say, "aw! Internet hugs!," and then pat themselves on the back thinking they've done enough (because for whatever reason, they're unable or unwilling to engage further). Get yourself comfortable with two facts: (1) This WILL happen, so you'll need to emotionally prepare for it and recognize that it's saying more about those people than it is about you, and (2) there WILL be enough people out there who have your back, and support will sometimes come from unexpected places if you show that you're open to it. You just have to take that first step and show that you're open to it.

If you've lost your job and you're upset and freaked out, that's very human and understandable. But you need to set a time limit for yourself about how long you let yourself feel that and be held back by it because the clock is always ticking, and your bills will show up next month whether you can afford them or not. If you're hesitant, start small…talk to just your family and your closest friends. When that goes okay, just enlarge the circle further and further from there. Nobody expects you to announce on social media that you're looking for work the day after you lose your job. Do it at your pace, at whatever pace is comfortable to you (while minding that ticking clock).

In 2021, I was part of a well-publicized case of a company mass firing dozens of developers. In a case like that, I felt it necessary to capitalize on the attention the story was getting by saying, "Hey, folks, I'm one of the folks hit by this" because top-of-mind awareness and sympathy for the developers involved was at a high point. So, that was one case where I DID announce immediately, before I'd really had time to emotionally process it…and doing that really paid off in the subsequent weeks. I wouldn't tell people to handle it this way in every situation, but it was a special case where speaking up immediately really helped. It doesn't even have to be in conjunction with bad news—maybe something you worked on has just been released, reached an important milestone, or has been nominated for an award—use that attention to your advantage. It's not sleazy to do that. It's what marketing people do for a living. What you're marketing is yourself.

You would get a lot of tags on Facebook and Twitter to check out job postings or calls for writers. (There were a couple of times I was going to tag you, and someone already had!) Did that surprise you at first?

Actually, yes, I was surprised at the response. It made me feel warm and fuzzy to know that I'd been thought of, and also that "what I do" was known well enough to people that they heard a certain type of opportunity come up, and they knew of me as someone who did that particular type of stuff. I don't think that would have been the case had I not been okay with talking publicly about the kinds of work I do and the kinds of things I'm looking to do.

During the time you were strictly freelance, how many of your gigs were from referrals or jobs that people in your network made you aware of?

I'm going to say 75–80%.

For a time, you included in your Twitter handle that you were looking for work. Were there other strategies or techniques you had to alert prospective clients that you were searching? Which of these did you find were most effective?

Flagging myself as "open to work" and "willing to hear from recruiters" on LinkedIn really helped. I'd say having a website and updating it are good moves too, but this last time, unemployment hit me while my site was down and being re-designed (still the case)! I guess just keep your website, your résumé, and your LinkedIn updated even when you're not looking for work because that can change overnight and, if it does, you're ahead of the game if you're immediately ready to start a search. Another strategy I had was to contact people I'd done work for before, who were satisfied with me…see if they've got anything they know of, see if they'll act as a reference, see if they'd write a testimonial. If they hired you once, they might again…and if that's not an option, then getting a reference or testimonial can help you going forward.

What advice would you give to freelancers who might feel embarrassed, feel like they're abusing relationships, or feel like they're pestering their friends if they ask for help?

Your friends are your friends because they care about you. They know you'd do the same for them if the shoe was on the other foot. They more than likely know how it feels to be looking for work, and how turbulent and competitive the industry is. Your biggest hurdle is likely going to be getting over shame, which is unfortunate.

I'd say that if you simply announce that you're looking for work and put up a reminder post every few weeks, that shows some self-awareness. As long as you're going about things humbly and gratefully with an eye toward not abusing relationships or annoying people, and you are constant in your effort to help others, you'll do great. I know of two contacts in the industry who inflate their experience, and only contact me to ask for favors, never to just say hi or send a silly meme or ask "How are you?" and never noticed (even saying "Wow, that sucks, I'm sorry, let me know if I can help") when I was in need. That's the kind of behavior that will make people roll their eyes when they even hear your name. Know the difference.

Remember to still be friends, still be human toward others, even outside of the job stuff. Talk to them sometimes without ever mentioning work, just to connect as people. It matters. The more you do that, without any expectations attached to it, the more people will have your back once you need their help because they know it's not the only reason you talk to them.

LESSENING (AND ELIMINATING) THE COMPETITION
Making Your Own Opportunities

I *hate* competition. I hate the thought that for any one job I apply for, there will be 100–200 other people vying for that same opportunity. (And, if the job is spread far and wide, there may be many more hundreds or even thousands applying.) I prefer it when I'm one of two or three options a prospective client has, or—you know—I'm the *only* option.

In an industry as competitive as games, where hundreds of qualified people can fight for one job, having absolutely no competition for a gig might sound fanciful. However, the scenario isn't all that unusual. In fact, most of the projects I work on now come with little to no competition. I did not have to apply for any of the gigs I got over the past two years (2019–2021).

My math might be a little off, but 99.9999% of games jobs are never made public. It might seem like the refrain of this book by now, but networking is key. When clients are looking to spend considerable money, they want to make sure that they can trust the people they're bringing on to their teams. They could publicly announce that they're looking for a writer, but what happens when they hire someone who can't do the job? And "can't do the job" could be for a lot of reasons. Maybe they did a great job on another game, but they can't get the voice down for *this* game. Maybe they think their ideas are more important than anyone else's, and they refuse to collaborate. Maybe, it turns out, they just can't do the work.

Not making any one job public avoids a lot of pitfalls when a client has lots of money on the line (and, sometimes, the future of the studio can also be at stake). It's much easier for the client to reach out to their network—people they've built relationships with and already trust—and ask for the names of freelancers who would be a good fit for their project. I regularly get e-mails or direct messages from friends and acquaintances asking me if I'm interested in a project or know if anyone who might be a good fit for a particular role.

Working Your Referrals

These referrals, the freelancer recommendations from their networks, have a much greater probability of getting the gig. Being referred doesn't mean you'll *automatically* be picked, unless you're the only freelancer who's referred for the job, and the client agrees you're the right fit.

This is why networking is so important. If you have a strong, supportive network, people know your abilities. When they hear friends or acquaintances are looking to fill certain roles, they will refer you because they *know* you. This is your network bearing fruit. And you may not see the benefits of having a supportive network right away. It might take months…or years. There are all sorts of variables to getting referred or not getting referred.

Building a network can feel like a transactional exercise—the reason you're developing these relationships is so your network can help you out. That *is* part of why you have a network. The key to being a good member of your network is to pay any support you receive forward. That could be in the form of referring someone else, giving advice, or any other way you can help advance someone else's career. Friends and acquaintances have referred me for jobs, and I've made referrals both on projects in which I've worked and when I get requests for referrals over e-mail or DM. The longer you work in the industry and the more people you get to know, the more opportunities you'll have to help someone else.

Don't Be Afraid to Ask for Help

Depending on your culture, upbringing, and personal philosophy, it may be difficult to say, "I need help." Being able to say, "I'm looking for work" or "I need help finding my next gig" is not a sign of weakness, especially not if you're in business for yourself and responsible for your livelihood. It's a **strategy** for finding work! How will your friends know you're looking for work *if you don't tell them*?

You can do exhaustive searches yourself. You can post to your social media channels that you're looking. But you're not going to reach everyone who might need your services. People in your network are connected to channels in which you aren't, and they have connections that you don't.

I have friends who regularly reach out to their networks and ask for referrals or to let them know about jobs they might not be aware of. My friends and I will always tag them on Facebook posts and tweets calling for applications. You probably have seen freelancers with "looking for work," "for hire," or something similar in their social media profiles.

Proving They Need You

Never underestimate the power of your own expertise. Being an active listener can alert you to potential work, even when your client isn't aware they may need someone with your services.

During the "What do you do?" part of the networking ritual, try going second in a one-on-one situation, or last or close to it in a group. This allows you to show your interest in whomever you're talking to, find out what their projects are, assess their needs, and think about how you might be able to help. You want to do more than just sell your abilities and list everything on your verbal résumé/CV. While people might find your experience and skills interesting, they're not really going to care about any of that if they can't apply it to their needs.

Ask the Right Questions

Remember that great questions invite great conversations. They're meant to engage. Ask thoughtful questions about what other people do, not just about how they might see a game writer or narrative designer being involved in a project. The right questions will demonstrate you're a great communicator and can get everyone else thinking in a collaborative environment.

When you're looking for work, questions mixed in with a little bit of your expertise will show your potential value, as well as get whomever you're speaking with to take into consideration what you're saying. For example, you meet the CEO of a start-up who's making an RPG...*in space!* You ask, "How are you developing your worldbuilding?" You'll quickly find out how much she knows about worldbuilding and how important this is to an RPG...*in space!* She tells you they've got a lot of the lore figured out, but they don't know how to include it into the plot. Based on her answers, you can have a conversation about how lore, worldbuilding, and game design influence each other in an RPG.

Now comes the part where you create a job for yourself. In that same scenario, you might ask if she has a narrative design team. She may say there are writers involved. This is where you explain the difference between the role of narrative design and writing in the game. You express interest in helping as a narrative designer. Or, perhaps, there are no writers or narrative designers. Nonwriters have been responsible for all of the storytelling. Again, you can express your interest and offer your services.

You may not have conversations where the prospective client's needs are that obvious, but this is why practicing active listening during networking (or even careful reading and asking follow-up questions over e-mail or social media[2]) is important.

In the last couple of years, for example, most of my jobs have been editing (substantive/developmental editing) and diversity consulting (which I consider a form of developmental editing). I achieved this because, as an editor, I've seen how desperately the game industry needs editors working with writers and narrative designers, and I've been able to communicate why. Where are the holes that need to be filled on particular projects, and how can you fill them?

There is the slight chance that the client will want to vet and interview more freelancers once you explain the services you offer and holes they need to fill on their teams. They get the idea from you and, as a reward, you might lose the opportunity you created to someone else. You have to think of yourself as a salesperson, not just a freelancer. You have to **close** and get the prospective client to commit to you.

Opportunities in Crowdfunding

Kickstarter and Indiegogo campaigns are other places where you can find work and potentially eliminate any competition in the process. Look for campaigns that have met their funding goals with time to go or are close to meeting them.

Find projects that specifically interest you and where you believe you'd be a valuable addition to the team. Contact the campaign creator, and see if they could use your services.

RESPONDING TO JOB POSTINGS

You can find postings in multiple places: Friends' Twitter and Facebook feeds, Facebook groups, Discord servers, discussion forums, etc. Keep in mind that because these job posting are public, there will be *many* applicants. Try to visualize for a moment the number of e-mails in the poor person's inbox who will have to read all of those applications.

Why is thinking about that person and the ungodly number of e-mails relevant? Because you will be adding to that person's work. And you, potentially, can be adding to that person's annoyance. Often, to get through all of those e-mails, people are looking for reasons to *reject* applications, not send them on to the next round. It's a lot easier to find flaws in the e-mail message or cover letter, the portfolio, or samples attached. Misspelling the contact name, not correcting typos, sending Word docs when they asked for PDFs, and sending four samples (because you just couldn't choose!) when they asked for three samples are all good ways to get your application rejected. It doesn't matter how talented you are or how perfect you would be for the job.

Before hitting send on your application, read the guidelines very carefully. Only submit what they ask for. If you don't have all of the experience or qualifications they're looking for, submit anyway. Now, do this within reason. If this is a senior-level job, and you've only worked on a couple of projects, this isn't the gig for you.

And this can't be said enough: Follow the f**king guidelines! The guidelines are not only there because they help prospective clients identify the right candidates, but they are also gatekeeping mechanisms. If someone can't follow the guidelines, could they follow instructions on the job? Would they actually be a team player?

I assisted one of my clients in looking for an artist. We were looking for a specific style. After reviewing several portfolios, we contacted three artists and asked them for a sample illustrating a scenario. One of the artists submitted something that was completely unconnected to the brief because they wanted to do "their own thing." You already know what happened to that submission. Not following the guidelines may say more about you than you realize. And if you abuse or ignore the system, you'll get a reputation and run the risk of being instantly rejected at the sight of your name or e-mail address. I would certainly never refer that artist to anyone.

ALWAYS proofread your e-mail carefully before you send it. As someone who's taught introductory writing courses and been a journal editor, I can tell you that there is an absolute correlation between mechanical writing errors and overall writing skill. The more typos and punctuation and grammar errors in a piece of writing, the less original and interesting it was. Is this always the case? No, but a few errors in a short e-mail message will signal to the recipient that maybe they shouldn't keep reading.

There are many reasons why someone might reject your application. Eliminate the unforced errors that will make it easy to not give you a second look.

The Art of Reading Listings

Not all job postings and listings you come across are worth your time. You might immediately recognize that you don't have the qualifications a prospective client is looking for or that the gig just doesn't interest you for any number of reasons. However, if a job *does* look like a good opportunity, scrutinizing the job description can give you insight into whom you might be working with—and if you actually *want* to work with them.

There's an art to reading job descriptions and queries and identifying good prospective clients. You might have a gut reaction that tells you it's worth it to try to get the client to respond to you. Other times, you're going to feel like you've been smacked in the face with red flags.

Some postings or correspondences are going to be full of information. Some might be only a couple of lines. Lack of information isn't a bad thing. It gives you opportunities to ask questions. Several clients I've worked with didn't have detailed information, but there was a confidence in the way that information was written.

Red flags can either point to a scam, a client who isn't really serious, or a project that's headed for disaster.

JOB POSTING RED FLAGS

- **No company affiliation.** Either the listing doesn't mention the company or client by name, or the person posting about the job (like on Twitter or Facebook) has no clear affiliation with the project, while acting as if they're associated with it. You want to know that you'll be working with a legitimate company.
- **Vague description.** What is it, exactly, that you would be doing? Does the prospective client seem to know? Maybe the client legitimately wants to hire someone, but if they don't have a clue what you'll be doing, you might end up in a situation that's structureless and disorganized. That disorganization extends from leadership, to lacking a concept and direction, to not having a clear schedule and goals, to missing payments. Those projects also tend to fall apart.
- **Lack of understanding your role.** This isn't always a bad thing. I've worked with clients who didn't know what narrative designers did, and I helped to flesh out my role on the project. However, when a client doesn't know the difference between a game designer and an artist, that says something about how (not) serious they are. (They couldn't be bothered to do the research on whom to hire.) When a client doesn't understand your skill set, they will have unrealistic expectations of you and your abilities.
- **Requesting free samples publicly.** The prospective client announces to a large group that they're making a game, and you should send your samples to the e-mail address listed. This is a great way for that person to get lots of free content. Think about it from the scammer's perspective: You have access to hundreds of writers or artists in a Facebook group or a Discord server. You post that you're looking to fill the position, and you give very specific details for what should be included in the samples. If at least 20 people respond, you've gotten a lot of content for your game for free. This is a scam I've seen writers fall for because they're eager for work.
- **Offering too-low rate.** This is another sign that (1) the prospective client has not researched how much the work should cost, or (2) the prospective client can't (or won't) pay for the value of the work. Either way, this is a red flag. Now, you might take on a job that pays very little because you believe in the project. But people who devalue the work tend to be nightmare clients.
- **Offering too-high rate.** "Too good to be true" is, well, likely true.

- **Typos and grammatical errors.** These point to a lack of professionalism. If you're trying to attract great talent, you want your information to be well written. Even when a prospective client posts about a job in a more casual environment over social media, they still want their messaging to be clear and engaging. Badly written job descriptions are flashing signs that the prospective client doesn't care about being professional, or they might not understand that they need to be.

QUERIES (YOURS AND THEIRS)

I mentioned that you might send a query to a crowdfunding campaign creator or prospective client unsolicited.[3] But how do you structure that letter, and what should you say?

Writing Query and Cover Letters

As is the case with all forms of writing, there's an art to writing query and cover letters. The most important thing to keep in mind, as I noted above, is that the person on the receiving end of your communication is looking for reasons to stop reading and reviewing.

Good queries are brief, but they need to address a few specifics.

The Client's Problem

All prospective clients have a problem that they need to be solved. The "problem," in this case, is the employer or client needs to make a game. They need to hire someone to work on a specific part of the game. When the prospective client needs a narrative designer or game writer on the team, this is the problem you're fixing. You need to explain how you are the right candidate for the job.

Keep in mind that you only have a short space to grab their attention (sometimes, this is literally a couple of phrases or sentences). You want to get to how you can help them ASAP.

So, for example, if it's a children's game, you might bring up the unique challenges of children's games (showing your expertise) and how you might address them.

Your Qualifications

State your expertise and qualifications *in the context* of this particular job. A lot of applicants make the mistake of listing their qualifications.

There are a lot of game writers and narrative designers out there. They're qualified for many jobs. But why are your qualifications relevant to this employer or client and their project? How can *you* help *them*? That's what they care about.

If you haven't worked on a game yet, you still have storytelling knowledge. Good storytelling is good storytelling, no matter the medium. You can point out your credentials as a writer.

Asking Questions

No description, listing, or initial communication will tell you all you need to know. You're going to have to ask questions of your own. Thoughtful questions illustrate your interest in the project.

Also, if you ask a question, you engage the reader. You're more likely to get a response because they have to send you an answer.

Don't overwhelm them with questions, however. It's been my experience that even when I ask three questions, I only get one or two of them answered. The important thing is to get them engaged and to keep them communicating with you. If you have questions that don't get answered, you can revisit them at another time.

TYPES OF QUESTIONS FOR QUERIES

Here are some questions you might ask the prospective client when you don't have a clear picture of the project or the freelancer's responsibilities:

- What is the game's genre?
- What is the game's setting?
- Who is the game's target demographic?
- How much of the story has been completed?
- What tone/style is the writing?
- When would your work need to be completed (what's the project timeline)?
- How many of the assets (art, animation, sound) have been created?

Sending Samples

Unless you're asked not to, *always* send samples. Your samples should be relevant to the project. If the game is humorous, send humorous samples. If it's a fantasy setting, send fantasy samples.

Sometimes you won't have any idea what kind of game it is. When this is the case, send up to five samples that show a range of what you can do. (Again, don't overwhelm them with lots of stuff to review.) Indicate that you'll send more on-target samples when you have a better understanding of the project.

Answering Questions/Responding to All Points

When the prospective client responds to your query, they'll probably have questions of their own. If you get questions like "How long will this take?," make sure you give an answer, even if you don't have enough information. You never want to leave a question unanswered, even if you have to say, "Can I get some more information?" Again, if you don't have enough information, ask follow-up questions.

Responding to all points raised in the job description/direct communication shows that you can follow directions!

Responding to Queries from Prospective Clients

It's a nice surprise when a prospective client unexpectedly reaches out to you. They'll usually find out about you from a referral, or they'll have reviewed your online portfolio. In my experience, these types of e-mails are introductory, with a short brief about the game, a short description of what they would need me to do, and a closing asking about my interest.

As is the case when you reach out to the prospective client, you're likely not going to have enough information to get a full understanding of the job, your role, or what the client needs from you. Sometimes, this is because you're not yet under NDA. Other times, it's because they may not know what information they need to give you. You're the expert, and they're going to need some of your guidance to help them flesh out the freelancer's responsibilities.

Since the client is interested in you and reaching out to you, you know you'll get responses to your questions. (Well, you're likely to get answers to your questions. There are times when you might not hear back from them...*ever.* Just an annoying part of the freelance life you have to get used to.) You'll probably get more specific details in their initial query, but similar questions as the ones under "Types of Questions for Queries" will apply.

BIDDING ON FREELANCING PLATFORMS

If you're using a freelancing platform to find work, you might find yourself having to bid for a job. A prospective client posts the job publicly or invites you to bid through a private query message. You then need to explain why you're right for the gig and place a bid with the rate you want for the job. Sometimes, you know what other people are bidding (Freelancer's bids are public, and Upwork shows the average bid and the highest and lowest bids).

Bid what *you* think the job is worth, not against other freelancers. When freelancers bid against each other, they end up driving the rate of the job down. You just need to keep your rates reasonable for your level of expertise and how complicated the job will be.

NEGOTIATING: GOING BEYOND PAY RATES

When you hear "negotiate," how much money you'll be fighting for probably comes to mind. However, negotiating entails so much more than that. In fact, other aspects of the negotiating process should determine your fee or the rate you'll ask for.

Negotiating isn't only important for determining what you'll be doing, for how long, and for how much, but it is also paramount for establishing your relationship on an equal footing with your soon-to-be client. Your client isn't dictating your work to you; you're going to come to an agreement on what that work is through negotiations.

Your Responsibilities

Your client will have ideas and some structure as to what your job will be. However, since you're the expert, you may recommend other duties or revise them. I've gotten into discussions with prospective clients who were looking for a game writer, but it became apparent that what they really needed was a narrative designer. They needed a world builder and someone to collaborate with artists on character and location designs, among other things.

Your responsibilities may also change once you're on the project, due to changes in budget, schedule, or limitations in technology. Once you and your client are aware that your responsibilities will change, you need to come into agreement on what these will be.

Your Schedule

Let the prospective client know how you tend to work when negotiating your schedule. If you will devote a certain number of hours a week to the job, be clear about this, and tell the client on which days you'll be available for meetings and other sessions. This is especially important if you're working more than one gig at a time. You'll need time to set aside for each of them and to be clear when your client can get in touch with you. So, if you're planning to work 20 hours a week, you might devote Mondays, Thursdays, and Fridays to that project.

You are going to have to be somewhat flexible. With international clients, you have to find times in your schedules that are compatible, or you will need to be up early or late. If you take the job, that's a sacrifice you have to make. But when you're just starting out, you might feel like you need to be available whenever your client wants to contact you. Fight that urge, though, and negotiate a firm schedule that includes when your client can expect to be able to communicate with you. Your client should never dictate to you when you should be working—that is something you and your client agree on.

What is the client's proposed timetable? Is it reasonable based on the work you need to do? Be specific about your timeline and why it will take as long as it will. If, say, the client wants you to write 20,000 words in a week (not at all hyperbolic that a client may think a writer can produce that many words in that short time), explain why this is unreasonable, how many words you can comfortably produce in a week, and when you would expect to have 20,000 words written.

If you're getting a fixed rate, you'll need to set up milestones for deliverables. There are several types of milestones:

- Milestones for turning in work.
- Milestones for receiving feedback from the client.
- Milestones for payment.

You and the client need to agree on the dates for these milestones. Also, make your client aware that you have to get feedback from them on the dates when that feedback is due. Any delays from the client, and that causes delays in your work.

Your Rate/Fee

This is based on the complexity of the work, your established rates, and how soon or not the client needs work done. If it's a rush job, the client should pay more for that. If the client is waffling on your ask, use professional organizations' suggested rates, and breakdown how you came up with your rates (what employed workers of your level of experience and responsibilities would make, etc.).

FREELANCING WHILE BEING EMPLOYED

There *is* another option to being solely a freelancer or solely having a salaried, permanent position. Individuals are able to successfully spend their time in both worlds. It doesn't matter why you might choose to do both: Maybe freelancing provides a creative outlet that your day job does not, or perhaps you need the stability of employment, but still want to take the odd freelancing gig.

Being a freelancer and employed at the same time is completely out of my realm of experience, so I will let a couple of freelancers who've done both at the same time take the stage.

 INTERVIEW WITH CHRIS TIHOR

Chris Tihor is a writer, game designer, and programmer, and partner at Talespinners, an outsource writing studio for games and immersive experiences. Most recently, he's worked as a story consultant on Nancy Drew: Midnight in Salem *for HeR Interactive, a story and narrative designer on* Agatha Christie: Hercule Poirot—The First Cases *for Blazing Griffin, and as the lead puzzle designer for the* Red Bull Mind Gamers: Puzzle Challenge, *as well as a number of other projects that he's not allowed to talk about yet. He firmly believes that every game should have cats in them that you can pet.*

What led you to pursue freelancing, instead of employment?

I'd been working as an employee for a number of years, and I'd had a few bad experiences working in toxic environments. When an opportunity arose to do some work on contract as a freelancer, I figured that I didn't have anything to lose by trying it out. I'm glad I did. I found freelancing allowed me to take more direct control over my career path, work environment, and day-to-day work habits.

In your professional life, you've had periods where you had permanent jobs, and periods when you were strictly freelance. Do you prefer one over the other?

Each situation has its pros and cons. Having a permanent job gives you a certain amount of stability. Generally, you know how much you're going to be earning financially for the foreseeable future, which helps greatly with planning a household budget. Also, employment often includes benefits, such as extended health coverage and paid time off. Freelancing, on the other hand, gives you a lot of freedom. As a freelancer, you're the one who makes choices about your day-to-day activities. You're suddenly running your own business and you have the freedom to make decisions about how it should be run. I think it's that freedom that I like the best.

Have there been times when you were employed part-time *and* freelancing? Do you find that easier or more difficult?

Actually, at the moment, I'm employed full-time and freelancing part-time. It's a good situation for me as my day job pays very well and offers benefits, and my freelancing gigs are creatively rewarding. The most difficult thing about this situation is that it can become very easy to get overloaded. I'm the kind of person that wants to do *everything*. I have many professional interests, I've worked as a programmer, game designer, and game writer among other things, and I have a ton of hobbies, as well. The problem is that I don't have the time or energy to do everything that I want to. I have to be careful not to commit to too many projects, or I become tired and cranky and, eventually, burned out. Maintaining a good work–life balance can be tricky at times, but it's absolutely vital for long-term health and happiness.

How do you know when it's time to search for employed work?

For me, the time to start looking for employed work is when your freelance income is no longer consistently covering your budgeted costs. Everyone, freelancer or employee, should have a household budget worked out. Seriously. It's a valuable tool to help you plan your life, and I'm surprised that it's not taught in schools more often. Your budget is a summary of all of your expenses: Rent, food, utilities, loan payments, and everything you need to pay for in a given month. Once you have a budget worked out, then you know how much money you need to be earning in order to cover your expenses for the month. Any time you're not able to cover your expenses with your earnings, you're going to have to dip into your savings, or worse, go into debt. This should be avoided. Once you start regularly dipping into your savings, it's time to start hitting the job boards.

How do you know when it's time to search for freelance work?

When working full-time: When my full-time job no longer seems worth the benefits, and my side projects are no longer satisfying enough, I know that I need to change something. That's when I start checking my savings situation and checking my contacts for any potential projects that might be a good match. Of course, sometimes things are going fine, and I'm minding my own business when suddenly a project pops up that I just can't refuse….

When working freelance: It's always the time to be searching for more freelance work. It's better to have more work you can handle (which you then pass along to fellow freelancers) than not enough work.

Has the switch between the two been easy or difficult? Is each time different?

Switching from employment to freelancing or vice versa can be difficult at times, largely due to the individual circumstances surrounding your transition. One time that I switched to employment from freelancing was especially difficult for me because I'd convinced myself that my current lack of work was due to a failure on my part. Freelancing gives you more freedom to make choices for yourself and your career, but it can also make you feel like you're responsible when things don't work out, even when it's because of things that are beyond your control. In this case, that was the trap that I fell into. My advice: Be aware of this and don't beat yourself up over "failures." Focus instead on the way forward and how to best plan for future successes.

Do you have to readjust to the "freelance life" or the "employed life," and how do you get yourself back into the right mindset?

Freelance life and employed life can be very different, depending on whom you're working for. Some workplaces treat their contract workers and full-time employees exactly the same, and some hold the two types of workers to very different standards. I've worked in places that look at freelancers as a necessary evil and others where they are esteemed as hallowed experts. The key, I think, to being successful in any of these situations is to make sure that you know what the expectations are for the people you're working for and take steps to meet or exceed them.

Do you have advice for anyone who's struggling with making the switch or wondering if they should (whether they're looking to go back to freelancing or searching for a permanent job)?

Freelancing: I suggest that, if possible, you start your freelancing career with a contingency fund in place. This would be savings sufficient to cover six months of your expenses. If you can't manage that, try to save as much as you can to start and put any earnings you have in excess of your monthly expenses into the fund until it hits your goal of six months of expenses. It seems like a lot but, trust me, you'll be thankful for it in the long run. Freelancing work generally goes in cycles of feast or famine, so a good habit to get into is paying into your contingency fund during times when you're earning more (feast) so that you can weather times when you're earning less (famine).

Permanent: Think about what aspects of freelancing that you enjoy the most, and see if you can find an employment situation that matches that as much as possible. For example, I enjoy being self-directed as a freelancer, so when I look for a permanent position, I try to find one that allows me to do that. The same applies to things you dislike. Hate having to manage project budgets? Find a position where that's someone else's job. Also, remember that you can negotiate with potential employers in the same way that you would negotiate with potential clients. You'd be surprised how flexible some employers can be, but you'll never know unless you ask.

 INTERVIEW WITH FRED WAN: THE FREELANCER

Fred Wan is a trial lawyer by day, and narrative designer and diversity consultant by night in both tabletop and digital spaces. His main areas of focus are giving players more ways to engage with and impact game worlds and each other, and using mechanics and narrative to strengthen each other. His best-known work was over a decade as one of the Story Leads for the tabletop brand Legend of the Five Rings, published by the Alderac Entertainment Group (now owned by Fantasy Flight Games).

When did you realize you could freelance part-time alongside your day job?

I was doing some writing on the side when I was still a student, so in one sense, I realized I could hold down the freelance side before I had my day job. I understood I could make it all work and juggle both after I graduated, while I was studying for my license, since I had to do both at the same time. By the time I had my license, I knew I could make balancing both work.

Why did you start freelancing part-time? Was it difficult to develop a schedule for your freelance writing at first? Did it get in the way of practicing law, or vice versa?

At first, the freelancing was mentally in the slot for "hobby that happens to make money rather than cost money," and was largely so I had an outlet to express myself. In that sense, it occupied "leisure time." At first, I simply stretched/crammed/worked longer hours to fit everything in, which wasn't the greatest solution in the long term. Eventually, in order to be reliable at both jobs, I became a bit more rigid and formal about sticking to certain hours for each and setting internal milestones, so I was staying on target for both.

I never found that freelancing got in the way of the day job—I kind of had to draw bright lines with the legal practice, and its obligations, coming first. That did mean turning down gigs I couldn't guarantee that I could deliver on.

How do you make time for both your day job and freelancing?

Weirdly, having to attend to both has forced me to be better about managing time at each. I remind myself that people are relying on me at both, which helps motivate me to stay focused, and have concrete days in mind to deliver on each.

How did you develop the discipline to make "space" for freelancing?

Largely, the freelancing work is a chance for me to exercise a part of myself that I can't as a lawyer. It's a lot easier to be disciplined about making space when you want to do it!

Are there times you have to turn down freelancing opportunities because of the day job? How do you know when it's time to turn a gig down?

Oh, many times, both in terms of applying and accepting. I generally look at it like this: If I get unexpectedly busy at the day job, will I still be able to deliver on this gig without having to crunch too much? Will future-Fred be sad because current-Fred accepted this gig? If the answer is "yes," then I turn the gig down.

Are there disadvantages to freelancing part-time? How do you overcome them?

The big one is that a lot of jobs out there want you to commit full-time hours for a number of weeks, rather than part-time hours for a number of months. I ask if there's any flexibility, or if I can frontload my portion of the work, so nobody is waiting on me. It doesn't always succeed, but it's worth trying!

What advice would you give to anyone who's thinking about freelancing part-time?

You're going to have to make trade-offs and sacrifices. Be aware of them. Consider what you want, and how important your day job, your freelancing, and your outside activities are to you, and budget your time. You want to make your decisions in an informed way. Even if they aren't perfect, you want to not be kicking yourself afterward for being foolish, brash, or inconsiderate to yourself and the people and things you care about.

What types of business structures are most fitting for part-time freelancing?

It varies a lot (and I'm not allowed to give legal advice outside of the day job)! Generally, you'll want to think about the administrative time and costs of each choice, as well as tax implications, and what kind of environment you want to work in. Get advice from people that you can talk to, and ask follow-up questions.

KEEP ALL AVENUES OPEN

Keep in mind that the competition for *any* job in games is high, including for the ones that are never made public. Have multiple approaches to your job search at all times. Also remember that some opportunities may come to you when you're not expecting them, and it may take a while for your networking to bear fruit. You may get those referrals right away. Or, as it was with me, it was several years before I started getting consistent referrals. And don't be afraid to reach out to your network to let people know you're searching. At any given time, there are plenty of opportunities they're aware of that you would never be able to find on your own.

EXERCISE

Crowdfunding Opportunities

Find a video game campaign that interests you on Kickstarter that's close to meeting its goal or that has already met its goal before the end of the campaign. Review all of the information on that project.

As a writer or narrative designer, how do you think you can help this project if you joined the team? List up to five ways you can benefit the team and the game.

Now, write a query letter to the person running the campaign. Make sure you go beyond asking, "Do you need a writer?" What can you offer as a writer or narrative designer? Why is that important to *this particular project*? You don't have to send the letter—this is just for practice.

However, if you would like to send the query, go to the campaign page, and click on the creator's profile. This will give you the creator's contact information or link to external sites where you can contact them.

NOTES

1. In other words, you won't engage in bad behavior, like harassing other members, being a troll, and engaging in hate speech. Yes, we're into the second decade of the 2000s, and this still has to be said.

2. Keep these conversations between you and the prospective client *in private*. You don't want to give onlookers the opportunity to jump into your conversations, start asking their own questions, and becoming your competitors for the job you're trying to create for yourself.

3. An unsolicited query, in other words, is when the prospective client isn't looking to fill a job and is not expecting to receive queries.

CHAPTER 12

Establishing Your Rates

The Eternal Freelancer Question

How much should my rates be?

Should I have different rates for different kinds of work?

Do I have a separate set of rates for developers who can't pay me as much, but I really believe in the project?

When do I raise my rates?

If I ask for my usual rate, will I price myself out of this job?

These are the questions that worry even veteran freelancers.

So, if you have fears or concerns that you're (1) not asking for enough or (2) asking for too much, know that figuring out what your rates should be is something freelancers constantly mull over.

This chapter will address what you'll need to consider when you're figuring out what your rates should be. We'll look at how your experience, education, and real-life expenses play factors. I'll give you the types of rates you might offer, like hourly, weekly, flat, etc. And I'll explain why knowingly asking for too little (lowballing) not only hurts you, but also hurts other freelancers.

DOI: 10.1201/9781003199779-14

But first, I have a confession to make. You can look up some great resources that will tell you how to figure out your rates. They'll give you industry standards and the average rates writers make in the industry. There are several good articles and documents you can find on this. I'll share them here. I've even written one.

At some point, however, these rate suggestions are going to be too low for someone of your experience and history. By the time you're experienced enough to get senior-level jobs at larger studios, these resources aren't going to be able to help you anymore. I have yet to see any of these sources list $100/hour as a *minimum* certain freelancers should be asking for.

How will you know when this time comes? That's hard to say. But if you feel like you've been stuck at a rate for some time, and you really feel like you should be making more, then that's probably it. An old tip freelancers give each other is: Did your client say "okay" right away? Then you didn't ask for enough. You may also have friends who will inform you, as mine did recently.

Does $100/hour *as a minimum* seem too high? Consider that all of the projects you've worked on, all of the ways you've learned how to collaborate with different personality types and learning styles, and all of the flexibility and versatility you've gained over the years are extremely valuable—not to mention the real-life expenses you'll have to account for in that $100/hour.

And if after reading this, you realize you need to start asking for at least $100/hour (or $2000 per week, etc.), know that you *will* find clients who know you're worth it!

WHY YOUR RATES SHOULD BE HIGHER THAN SALARIED RATES

In the United States, employers take taxable income out of their employees' income on their behalf. If you are a freelancer, you have to pay this taxable income yourself. Employers also take care of certain benefits for their employees, like health insurance. Because you're acting as your own employer, you're having to make payments that are added expenses for you, and not employees. You should take this into account as to why you need to make more than someone on a salary.

A good rule of thumb is to ask for twice that of salaried rates.

INTERVIEW WITH SHEL KAHN

Shel Kahn has worked in indie video games as an art director, concept artist, and 2D artist since 2011; they've worked with small teams on console, PC, and mobile games, including Numizmatic's Light Fingers. *Kahn has also worked with a range of publishers on pen and paper games, as well as fantasy and memoir comics, and they have presented and taught at professional conferences, as well as at high schools, colleges, and universities. Kahn's passion projects include self-publishing comics and tabletop RPG modules, teaching literacy through tabletop RPGs, and community organizing.*

What led you to pursue freelancing, instead of employment?

For me, it was largely tied to my choice of industry—illustration and vis dev have a lot of freelance opportunities, much more than they have full-time salaried gigs available at any one time. I actually started taking on small freelance jobs while I was still in school, which led to me going part-time with school, which led to me transitioning fairly seamlessly into freelancing.

Freelancing remained really appealing to me because I love working on a variety of different projects, and the shorter-term projects really let me feel excited about work every day. I also get to spend some of my time on being an independent creator and self-publisher in comics and games, and doing educational and community projects, and getting to choose when to shift to prioritizing those and when to shift back to client work has been really good for me.

At this point, it's been a decade, and I'm not really sure I'd know how not to freelance!

Coming up with rates causes a lot of angst and anxiety for freelancers. How did you get the confidence to ask for what you believed your work was worth?

So, as I mentioned, I've been working freelance for a decade; after about five years of freelance, I had steady clients and was constantly busy, but I noticed that I was not meeting my own financial goals—or even my financial needs, really. Around that time, I also started losing working hours in the day to health issues and chronic pain, and I realized that I needed to squeeze a lot more financial value out of each hour of my day. Since I was now turning down some jobs due to reduced time, I felt like I could probably get away with raising my rates, and I knew that if I wanted to stay in this field, I'd have to. So, it was less a feeling of confidence and more a feeling of "if this doesn't work, I am in a lot of trouble," haha! The confidence came after I successfully did raise my rates a little; it created momentum for me to keep raising them as I needed to.

There are a lot of different resources for freelancers to figure out what their rates should be. What information and sources have you used to establish your rates?

This was for sure the biggest challenge at the beginning of my career!

Some clients offer fixed rates when they reach out with a job, and those rates *may* be negotiable, but often with one-off pieces for bigger companies, the rates are take-it-or-leave-it. These gigs were a great way to get a sense of what was being offered, but they are usually not the best rates available, in my experience; so I started out just matching them and then did more research.

Places I did that research: The Graphic Artists Guild pricing guide was a great place to start, but I found it rarely had numbers specific to the exact industries I was working in. I also made a lot of use of a website called art-PACT that was a rate-sharing and client-rating resource for freelance artists. Unfortunately, it's since dissolved, but similar efforts pop up from time to time and are always worth taking a good look at.

Some of the most helpful things I've done are to connect with other folks at my level in the industry and talk to them frankly about rates. It becomes obvious that rates can vary hugely by client and project, and that kind of made it feel easier to say, "No, I won't work for under X amount anymore."

And Google does have info if you go digging, but it's never as well vetted as the other sources I mentioned, so take it with a grain of salt.

Nowadays, I have a decade of time tracking to refer to when a client asks me how much something will cost, so I can usually estimate fairly closely how long a particular assignment will take me, and this helps me do the math of "what do I need to earn to live and save some money and get bubble tea sometimes" and then work backward from there to make sure my rates reflect that.

When was the first time you realized you needed to raise your rates?

I mentioned to an illustrator friend that I was working on color illustrations for $50/each and their jaw dropped to the floor. Their frankness really helped me reassess what my time and work was worth.

You have a particular strategy for incrementally raising your rates. How did you come up with it? By how much do you increase your hourly rate each time?

So, I have two types of rates: Piecework, which is a flat fee rate for single pieces of art, that I use for things that are first and foremost illustrations; and hourly, which is for a longer working relationship, particularly doing concept art or art direction for games.

With my hourly rates, I've increased them in increments of $5 or $10 at a time, so no huge jumps at once! This kind of slow but steady approach helped me be cautious, see what my clients were comfortable with, and not make huge changes at once.

With my illustration rates, the increment can jump much faster if I have evidence that there's room to get paid more—that evidence can be: Getting hired by a BIG company, getting headhunted aggressively, getting a wake-up call from a fellow freelancer. If I am not certain, I'll keep my increment smaller, but I do try to continuously increase my rates, at least little by little.

And my main way to tell if I am able to raise my rates is when a client agrees to my quote a little too enthusiastically, with no hesitation or negotiation. That tells me that there is potentially room to negotiate a little higher, and I make note of this for the next time I have to quote a client. This has not failed me so far.

How often do you raise your rates?

It definitely depends on the type of project, but with hourly rates, I raise them usually with each new *big* project. So a year where I'm art directing at $55/hr makes me feel confident that I can charge $60/hr the next time I get picked up for a big gig.

With illustration projects, I definitely try and raise my rates with each new client, and if that goes well, I usually end up updating repeat clients, as well. Again, these increments are usually quite small, so I'm not blowing my own mind with my income right now, but I do feel like I can see how to get there eventually, and that's both exciting and a relief.

Based on your strategy for raising your rates, you mentioned raising them on your repeat clients. How did you inform them that your rates were increasing? How did they respond?

Often, repeat clients e-mail offering work, so I would reply, "Yes, but heads-up, my rates went up" and include an estimated quote for the new gig; sometimes they don't say anything besides "sure"; sometimes they say "that's outside of our budget" or something similar. I try to be prepared for both outcomes.

I have never had any professional client cuss me out over it. I hear about nightmares from folks who do more private commissions, but those rates are a whole other thing that I unfortunately do not have any experience with.

So, yes, I have lost clients, but it's not personal. Projects I used to be involved in have not been able to pay me my new rates, but I try to find new clients regularly and fill those voids, and that lets me not feel it too intensely when a client turns down my quote.

What advice would you give to freelancers who might be nervous about raising their rates?

First up: It's worth it! It's so worth it! Remember, you're worth it!

Practical advice first: Try it with a new client who sought you out first, and mention it to repeat clients next time they approach you—in both situations, these are times when clients are excited about working with you and thus see your value, and you're going to have more power in the negotiation than if you are cold-emailing a new or existing client.

If you need to break it to repeat clients gently, a "my rates are going up, but I'll do *one-last-gig* at the old rate with you because you've been so great" e-mail is a very nice way to break the news to them and let them know for next time, while still keeping the working relationship. This can be a bit of a trap if you keep extending the one-last-gig, so only use it in situations where you need to take the job either way and are really worried about them having an upper limit to their budget. Honestly, most clients I've emailed have been very happy to have an honest negotiation or discussion of their budget limitations.

But first and foremost: Find ways to convince yourself that you are worth the money! Whether it's being wedged between a rock and a hard place when it comes to workable hours and cost of living, which I admit was a bit drastic for me, or whether it's talking to other pros about their rates and getting their advice on where you might price yourself based on your work, use those situations to remind yourself why this is worthwhile to you and for you. Remember that while you may have a person-to-person relationship with your clients, they and you are also both businesses, and rates are a business negotiation, not a personal thing at all.

And honestly, corporations' C-level execs are legit legally required by common law to prioritize the corporation's profits, and while you might not be a corporation, you are also allowed to prioritize your own profit now and then. It's not like anyone's giving us a great retirement fund; we have to build security for ourselves as freelancers.

And in the end, you are allowed to earn more than the bare minimum; you deserve to find a way to comfort, security, and satisfaction. Freelancing is a hard enough quest without the imposter syndrome keeping you from earning what you need!

What advice would you give to freelancers who might be nervous about losing their clients if they raise their rates?

You *will* lose some clients. People have fixed budgets, and sometimes that means getting higher rates from them isn't possible. And, yes, some people are jerks, and there are a lot of systemically reinforced reasons some clients will think they can get away with paying you less than other people. You can't fix them, but you do get to set your own boundaries, and in my experience, new clients who will pay you higher rates will be worth the work of searching out.

Consistently, I have found that clients who are paying me more treat me more professionally. Quoting a higher rate definitely feels like walking into the negotiation as three kids stacked up in a trench coat but, to the client, I think it can actually make you look more like a confident professional who knows their worth.

Clients who are offended by this new you were never going to be particularly respectful. Clients who were wonderful to you even when you were charging lower rates will not be jerks about you raising them—they'll understand, even if their budgets prevent you from working together again.

In the end, continuously keeping an eye out for new clients is the best way to feel secure as a freelancer, and it's the best way to raise your rates.

ESTABLISHING RATES AND FINDING WORK

And now for that popular question: How much do I charge? I'll tell you what you *don't* want to do first, and that's lowball.

DON'T LOWBALL (SERIOUSLY, DON'T DO IT)

Lowballing is working for a ridiculously cheap rate when the job is worth a lot more. There are freelancers who are willing to work for what turns out to be less than $1 per hour, or they'll write 25,000 words for 20 bucks.

Reasons why people lowball:

- They need experience because they're new to freelancing and are trying to establish themselves.

- They figure clients will be more likely to hire them if they're cheap; they can build up their experience and then raise their rates.

- They just don't know how much they should charge.

Clients take advantage of these contractors, or they don't know what the work is worth themselves. (In many cases, people think, "Hey, anybody can write! It's not like it's some valuable skill!")

Good clients will equate your skill with the low price. You're cheap, so your work must be cheap, too. Cheap rates = cheap work.

LOWBALL, AND THE CHEAPSKATES WIN (OR DON'T SCREW WITH MY MONEY)[1]

There are serious dangers to lowballing.

You may find it's difficult to raise your rates, especially if you're on a freelance site, and prospective clients can view your job history and how much you charged. They might be suspicious of you trying to raise your rates on them, when you were so very, very cheap before.

You may lose your repeat clients because they won't be willing to pay you at your new rates when you do decide to raise them.

You screw up everybody else's cash flow—including mine and that of all the other freelancers out there. When clients really don't know what they should be charging, it becomes difficult for others to earn higher rates because clients have grossly unrealistic expectations. (In short, don't screw with other people's money.)

ESTABLISHING RATES[2]

Your rates should be determined by your education in the field, your work history in the field (or related fields), your work history with clients, and going market rates.

If you're freelancing full-time, or if freelancing makes up most of your income, you need to keep your living expenses in mind. How much do you need to earn in a year? How much do you need to make in a month? What bills do you need to pay? These can include the following:

- family needs,

- rent,

- groceries,

- car payments,

- student loans,

- other debts, and/or

- business expenses.

The Freelance Hourly Rate Calculator, an online resource, can help you figure out a minimum based on your goals and expenses: http://allindiewriters.com/freelance-hourly-rate-calculator/.

Please note that you should include in your overall fee meetings you attend and any time for research or prep work for the job. This includes brainstorming, jotting down notes on paper or digitally, and looking up information that will help you or your team.

The Minimum Acceptable Rate

When you're looking at minimums, they should be based on established professional rates. These are rates that *professional organizations* have declared to meet professional standards. Start with the minimum professional rate, and add to it based on your level of experience in the industry and with adjacent industries and your educational background. For example, you may have worked on one game, but if you have a degree in creative writing, film writing, English, or literature, you have more foundational knowledge about storytelling than someone who's worked on one project and has a degree in computer science.

WHERE TO FIND PROFESSIONAL RATES

There's only one professional organization that has published recommendations for game writing and narrative design rates, and that is the Writers' Guild of Great Britain. Other resources are industry adjacent. While they might not state what game writers should make, you can look at the types of writing they list and find a comparable writing task in games. If you're not a writer, you can also look up the organizations' recommendations for professional artists, programmers, musicians, etc. When necessary, convert these suggestions to your country's currency.

RECOMMENDED RESOURCES

- "Videogames Guidelines," Writers' Guild of Great Britain: https://writersguild.org.uk/videogames-guidelines/
- "Editorial Rates," Editorial Freelancers Association: https://www.the-efa.org/rates/
- *Writer's Market: How Much Should I Charge?* (A survey of professional writers): https://www.slideshare.net/modwilli/writers-market-how-much-should-i-charge

A HARD TRUTH OF ONLINE FREELANCING

Many freelancers, including successful, established ones, make less online/virtually than they do onsite, unless their client is a large corporation or a AAA publisher. That doesn't mean that you can't earn $50/hour or more or make $1000 and up writing documentation.

TYPES OF RATES YOU CAN OFFER

You can be paid hourly, daily, or weekly, and get paid through milestones with a fixed rate. You can be flexible with rates. On one project, you may go with an hourly rate. On another, you and a client may agree to a weekly rate. Some freelancers only use one type of rate, period. Sometimes, the client will not give you a choice as to how you wish to be paid.

Here's a breakdown of rates and why you might choose them over others for different jobs.

Hourly Rate

With an hourly rate, you get paid a certain amount per hour you work.

Disadvantages: If you're a fast writer, you're not going to make as much hourly as you would a daily, weekly, or fixed rate. Your speed and efficiency are actually to your detriment. Clients may pressure you for the number of hours you will take because you might "take too long." (Translation: The job will start costing too much.) Without warrant, they may feel you're taking advantage of them, especially if they were not able to give you clear information to figure out a time frame before you took the job.

I view certain types of jobs as *input* centric and *output* centric. To me, rates are also input or output centric, based on the job. For example, coding is an inputting discipline. The programmer inputs and corrects as much code as needed until the job is done. On the other hand, disciplines like writing and art are output centric. The point of writing a bible or drawing concept art for characters is to create finished products. For the same reason, editing isn't output centric because it's not about producing a finished product. It's inputting edits on a finished product.

However, the type of rate you choose should be based on *your business, the project, and the client.*

Advantages: Hourly rates are good if you can (1) estimate the total number of hours for a project and (2) know that your hourly rate would net the same as a daily (8-hour workday) or weekly rate (20 hours at the least). Hourly rates are also beneficial if you're on a longer-term gig that will take at least a few months.

Daily Rate

This is the amount you will make per day on a project. Freelancers usually determine this rate by their hourly rate and how many hours they work in a day.

Disadvantages: Daily rates can be pricier for some clients, as they're based on an 8-hour workday. They may not be feasible for longer projects.

Advantages: A daily rate makes a lot of sense for shorter jobs, especially if you know the number of days you'll be working with the client. It's also good when you're brought in for a project to give your expertise. For example, the client might hire you as a narrative consultant, and you take two or three days to review the script. You can also add a daily rate to a job if you need to travel. You're telecommuting, and you're working on a fixed rate. But you travel to the studio for a couple of days. The daily rate covers your travel expenses, as well as your work for those days.

Weekly Rate

You are paid a certain amount for each week you work on a project. Freelancers usually determine their weekly rate by multiplying their hourly rate by the number of hours they intend to work per week. So, if your hourly rate is $50, and you will work 20 hours a week, your weekly rate is $1000.

Disadvantages: A weekly rate may not make sense for a smaller project or when you go long periods without delivering work. For example, you have two months on your schedule to turn in a game bible, and you won't be spending every workday of those two months on the document. Payment via milestones or an hourly rate would make more sense.

Advantages: If you have a lot of work on a project and will be spending your work week on it, a weekly rate covers your activities and responsibilities. For example, not only are you writing, but you're also in meetings throughout the week. This is like an hourly rate, except you multiply the hourly rate by your total hours for the week.

Flat or Fixed Rate

For a fixed rate, you and the client agree on the total cost of the job before you sign your contract. You are then paid via milestones throughout your time on the project.

There are several techniques for determining the fixed rate for a project:

- Estimate the number of hours you believe the project will take. Multiply those total hours by your hourly rate.

- Analyze employee salaries at studios. What are game writers and narrative designers with your level of experience and qualifications making per year? Figure out how much they make per month. Based on how long your job is, you can break this down even further: per month, biweekly, per week, per day, etc. Now, include the expenses you have to pay out of pocket as a freelancer, everything an employer doesn't take care of for you, plus your living expenses.

- Come up with fixed rates for the types of work you do. So, for example, you have a flat rate for scripts of a certain length, you have a rate for a game/story bible, etc. Again, there are several ways you can determine what your rate for each will be.

Disadvantages: You can end up working way more and not being paid enough for it. This can be due to scope creep, if your responsibilities continue to be expanded and you don't renegotiate what you need to be paid for the extra work. You can underestimate how long the project will take, and you end up working for less than your hourly rate. Also, if it's not a longer project, it wouldn't make sense to break the project up into milestones.

Advantages: If you write quickly (like me), you can put a value on the work and not rely on an hourly rate, which might cause you to make way less than you assess it to be worth. The fixed rate focuses on the *output*, and the client won't get anxious about you working too many hours and when you'll finish.

There's No Consensus

It's up to you whether you charge by the hour or establish a fixed rate. Freelancers have varying opinions on this. Some only get paid by the hour. Some get paid a weekly rate based on their hourly rate. Others have a fixed rate, especially if the job won't take them very long, and they'd end up making very little on the hourly rate. As you figure out your financial needs, determine what payment option makes the most sense for you.

Per-Word Rates

Writers should avoid per-word rates—with some exceptions. Per-word rates are common when you're selling short stories, novelettes, or novellas. However, they don't make sense in games for a couple of reasons:

1. Games tend to use *fewer* words. A per-word rate would not reflect on the amount of work you put into the project.

2. Clients might be concerned you will try to pad your words (add unnecessary words) to make more money.

You *can* come up with a fixed rate based on the number of words, if you know the number of words your client's assigned to you. We'll look at a scenario for this in a bit.

The only professional organization to set a minimum acceptable per-word rate is the Science Fiction & Fantasy Writers of America (SFWA). As of 2021, SFWA's minimum rate is 8 cents per word USD. Now, that's not very much at all. You might be wondering why I said there are times where you might come up with a fixed rate based on a project's number of words.

I recommend looking at the word rates of "slick" magazines, newspapers, and other publications with large audiences. They have bigger budgets, as compared to some smaller publications paying 8 cents. So, 25 cents per word would be on the lower end for larger publications. Some magazines pay as much as $1 or $2 per word!

You can use a site like XE.com to find the rate in your country's currency.

When the Per-Word Rate Makes Sense

I very respectfully and very strongly disagree with veteran freelancers who say you should never go with a per-word rate over an hourly rate.

When your client gives you a fixed word count or minimum to maximum number of words, a flat rate can be more profitable.

Here's a very real scenario you may find yourself in. More and more developers are publishing interactive fiction apps. These are apps like Chapters, Choices, and Episodes, and the games are visual novels. They're text heavy with branching narrative and choices. Devs and investors new to the genre usually know how long they want a play session to be, and they'll give you an expected word range for each story. What they tend *not* to know is how much to pay writers for the scripts. When they approach you to write for them, they expect you'll be able to tell them a good, professional rate for the work.

(It's important to note here that some devs publishing interactive fiction have established a fixed rate for each script, and you may not be able to negotiate your rate.)

So, a prospective client tells you they'd like you to write a 30,000-word script for their interactive fiction app. I'll break down what an hourly rate and a fixed rate would net you. Let's say you're a veteran writer. Your hourly rate is $100. You suspect you could turn around 30,000 words in 30 hours (1000 words per hour) or 40 hours (750 words per hour).

But you're also considering going with a fixed rate. Let's use a rate I actually got for a 30,000-word script: US$10,000. That's 33 cents per word, for the record.

In this case, would you prefer your hourly rate or a fixed rate of $10,000?

You're forgiven if you're yelling "I'm a writer, not a mathematician!" right now. Here's a breakdown:

$100/hr for 30 hours = $3000

vs.

$100/hr for 40 hours = $4000

vs.

$10,000 for 30,000 words.

If you went with your hourly rate instead of the fixed rate, you would lose between $6000 and $7000.

Let's make the time frame for completion a bit more generous. It's going to take you 60 hours to write 30,000 words:

$100/hr for 60 hours = $6000

vs.

$10,000 for 30,000 words

You're still selling yourself short by $4000.

Now, let's say your hourly writing rate is $150 per hour:

$150/hr for 30 hours = $4500

vs.

$150/hr for 40 hours = $6000

vs.

$150/hr for 60 hours = $9000

vs.

$10,000 for 30,000 words.

Of course, $150 per hour is better, especially if you need 60 hours to complete the job. But what if you write faster than that? What if writing

30,000 words would take you considerably less time? The fixed rate of $10,000 is still the way to go.

Of course, you could be thinking, "Ha! If my hourly rate's $200 an hour, and I take 60 hours, that would get me $12,000! Better than that $10,000 fixed rate!" Yes, that is indeed true.

And you are, no doubt, drooling at the thought of making $12,000 for 60 hours of writing.

But now it's time to throw a little bit of reality into this scenario. Except for one, every interactive fiction project I've worked on had a quick turn-around. Development of these games is *expected* to go quickly. With interactive fiction, a client can get a lot of content in a shorter period of time because its text is heavy with much fewer assets. Sometimes, your client will tell you up front how many hours they expect the job will take. (Read: They're going to work with freelancers who agree to those hours.)

In the case where you don't have much time, you *really* should get all the money you can out of a gig, especially considering how much mental and physical energy you'll have to exert—and that you're creating IP for someone else.

So, with realistic expectations in mind, would you rather go with your hourly rate or a fixed rate, when you can name your price?

One last point on this scenario of a fixed rate based on a known and firm word count: You want to break up the payments of that $10,000, especially if the project is drawn out, and you won't be paid quickly. In other words, "quickly" would be you finish the project within a couple weeks, deliver the script, and get paid within 2 weeks or less.

The process can be drawn out for a number of reasons: You're writing a couple of revisions, you have to wait for client feedback before you can implement those revisions, and/or the client can take a month or longer to pay you once you've turned in the final version of the script. You can go a long time without being paid. Consider getting paid some of that fixed rate up front. You can also get paid some of that fixed rate with milestones.

THE RIGHT RATES ARE GOOD FOR YOUR MENTAL WELL-BEING

It's important you're paid what you're worth in order to have a life, but it's also important because you won't be miserable when you realize you were underpaid.

WHEN TO CHANGE YOUR RATES

As you gain more experience in the industry and work on more games, you have the right to raise your rates. As I mentioned earlier, when your rates accurately reflect your professional experience, it's good for both you and other people in the industry. Clients need to understand what professional rates are, and freelancers are partly responsible for establishing them.

Raising rates are one of those things in the freelance life that causes stress and anxiety—just like establishing rates to begin with. Here are questions you might have (they're common to every freelancer!):

Q: How do I know I'm ready to change my rates?

A: As I said earlier, you might get the sense that you're "stuck." You've been at the same rate for several years, and you've become more of an expert over that time. "Expert" doesn't only mean that you've been a writer or narrative designer on several titles. It also means that you've worked with different workflows, have probably sometimes been in leadership positions, and have developed your collaboration skills.

Are you making junior-level rates, and you have mid-level expertise? Or you're making mid-level rates, and your experience is comparable to people in the industry at a senior level? Then it's time to think about raising your rates.

Q: Will I lose my repeat clients if I raise my rates on them?

A: Yes, you might lose some of them, to be blunt. They may not be able to afford you anymore. They may simply choose not to pay you and find someone cheaper. It's never easy to lose clients you've been working with on several projects, especially when you trust each other in the collaborative relationship.

If you think you might lose some clients when you raise your rates, try to find some new clients who will pay your new rates first. If and when you lose your old clients, you won't be left without money coming in.

Q: How do I tell my current clients I'm raising my rates?

A: Be honest, even though money talk can be hard. Let them know why you're raising your rates.

How you want to handle your current clients is up to you. You might grandfather them in to your old rates. You may do the next couple of projects at the old rates, and then you'll raise them. That gives them time to get over the shock of having to pay more and gives them the opportunity to get the funding for your new rates.

INTERVIEW WITH C.J. KERSHNER

C.J. Kershner is a writer and the head of Polyhedron Productions, an independent studio based in New York.

What led you to pursue freelancing, instead of employment?

This may be arguing semantics, but I consider myself employed, just not by a publicly traded multinational corporation. Is self-employment different than freelancing? I think so. Our clients contract the narrative development services we provide through the LLC I founded, but that's only one part of our overall business (and there's a lot more could be said about setting all that up—bank accounts, company credit cards, insurance, etc.).

As for why I left a staff role at a larger company for the uncertainty of starting my own, there are two reasons.

The first is that I craved novelty at a studio in which the dominant paradigm was to attach writers to established brands for multiple entries/sequels in a series. I liked to bounce around, work on different types of games in different genres, and grow by exploring skills and subjects outside my current experience. There's nothing wrong with the way it operated—in many ways there were clear benefits (team cohesion, for example)—but leaving meant I could be free to pursue a variety of projects rather than buck the cultural pressure to fit in and stay put. I'm proud to say, to date, I've never made the same thing twice (or at least not twice-in-a-row).

The second reason is that when I spoke out against a hate group that was targeting my colleagues on social media—though opinions were clearly stated as my own, it mentioned the project outside accepted marketing talking points, which I admit was my fault—and said hate group told the company it should fire me*; the company tried to do just that. The administration demonstrated it was ready to do whatever it took to put out the PR fire. In the end, it legally couldn't, but it was clear I was no longer welcome. I started making my exit plans, so that by the time a random associate producer proposed I be demoted, I had already given my two weeks' notice.

*They also said: I should kill myself; they would kill me (and provided video evidence they could); they hoped I—and everyone in my immediate family—would be sexually assaulted or spontaneously die from other causes. Both the company and the police were deaf to these statements.

How do you determine your rates? Do you have a preference for hourly, weekly, by milestones, etc? Or do certain factors like the project, scheduling, your role, etc., dictate the rate?

I wish I knew how I determined my rates!

Previously, if I extrapolated my base hourly (which was $65 per) out to an annual salary [(40 hrs/week) x (52 wks/year)], it seemed it would be more than sufficient to cover living expenses in most parts of the United States, with enough left over to save and/or spend on nonessential expenses. Of course, independent contracting doesn't work like that, but coming from a salaried position, I didn't know any better and quoted that as my default for years.

On projects lasting less than three months, I'm open to exploring a flat fee with a clear schedule of deliverables and iterations, but in general I try to negotiate for a fixed weekly rate. In my experience, the number of hours tends to fluctuate—sometimes it's a trickle and others a flood—and milestones might shift, so a decent weekly expectation helps pad the slow spells (you still get paid a livable rate when there isn't as much to do for reasons outside your control) and justify the fast ones (within reason).

When do you know it's time to raise your rates?

Again, I wish I knew.

Does it sting when I hear about others earning orders of magnitude more, either hourly or as consulting fees, perhaps because of their name recognition or past (sometimes distant past) accomplishments, while it feels like I'm doing the day-to-day heavy lifting?

Yeah, it does.

Does it smart when I hear what my friends are earning at big studios in relatively stable full-time positions, with health care and tax deductions taken care of by an entire accounting department, even if their cost of living is through the roof because they're in an urban development hub where "affordable housing" is 50%+ of their take-home?

Yup.

Could I perhaps be charging a higher rate, given my years of experience, awards and nominations, and plethora of shipped titles with solid sales and review scores?

Sure.

And the next contract that comes around maybe I'll try to do just that, and maybe the client will agree to the amount...or maybe they won't. But, as long as I can pay for my everyday expenses, maybe that's okay? Thankfully, I learned early to save aggressively for the lean times and to get a CPA to utilize every advantage come tax time.

Meanwhile, there's a large percentage of the population who aren't as privileged working long hours in hard conditions for minimum wage (or less) who still can't make ends meet and I'm getting paid *how much? To write video games?* And I'm going to try to demand more? No, no, it's okay. When the revolution comes, I'll see myself to the wall, thank you.

Has there ever been a time when you realized you could have asked for more, and the client would have been fine with it?

In my experience, it's been less an issue of realizing I could have asked for more and more of realizing I wasn't charging for the fully agreed upon amount in the first place. For example, on one early contract, the services to be provided were for a fixed fee, which the client agreed to pay out in weekly installments ($50k for 10 months, part-time); however, I only invoiced them for hours worked, which was often under that weekly amount (I was still learning the ropes of running a business while simultaneously doing the job). At the conclusion of that contract, there was a large amount (~$20k) that hadn't yet been invoiced, but since the services had all been performed, the client was hesitant to pay out the remainder. In the end, they agreed to pay half the outstanding balance, but if I'd billed according to the original terms, I would've collected the entire amount.

While I wish I could say "lesson learned" after that experience, I made a similar mistake on a recent, more lucrative, contract, where the payments for hours worked at the hourly rate were far below the originally proposed budget for services. And that's why I hired an accounts manager.

A huge factor freelancers need to consider when they're thinking about what their rate will be is the time they'll be on that job, and if the client's proposed timetable is reasonable. Do you have strategies or processes for determining how long your commitment to a job might be?

If the client doesn't set a fixed schedule during the contract negotiation phase (these tend to be the larger, shorter-term, higher-yield jobs), then I assume I'll be on the project long-term, and it behooves me to propose a renewal period, usually every six months to a year. A few weeks before that deadline, I'll call a meeting where the client and I review and/or update the statements of work, add new ones if needed, and amend the main service agreement with another date in the future for the next review. In these cases, I try (but am not always successful) to push for a weekly or monthly rate to ensure my own living expenses are met, the business is sustainable (monthly burn rate for staff, utilities, software licenses, etc.), and there's enough left over to save.

It's also worth taking time to examine the terms for termination and propose adding a kill fee, in case anything should go wrong (and for which the fault is not mine).

As for the reasonableness of clients and their proposed timetables, even the ones that seem solid often tend to shift (15k lines in 3 months can suddenly become 25k in 6 months as the design on their end changes); again, this is where terms in the contract should be inserted to accommodate this possibility and ensure I get fair compensation (or where the fixed weekly fee comes in handy).

In rare cases where one contract is ending just as another is beginning, it pays to set terms early about passing along work to employees or subcontractors should there be any outstanding work (again, for which the cause is not mine). Most freelance contracts forbid this, but it's worth bringing up in the initial discussions if it seems like it could potentially happen.

Have you ever had to negotiate your rates, schedule, and responsibilities? What is your strategy for that? When do you know it's time to walk away if you and the prospective client haven't come to an agreement?

Strangely, the agreements where I had to negotiate (vs. simply propose a higher rate or detail a different deliverable schedule) and the ones which I walked away from were over seemingly minor points.

For example: One client, based in the United Kingdom, demanded my studio provide £1m of liability insurance; being US based, our liability coverage at the time was $1m. Given the exchange rate, they wouldn't accept the lower amount, and the cost to match it would exceed the earnings from the contract, so we apologized for being unable to meet their needs and took our leave. If I had represented myself solely as a freelancer, those terms would not have been present, but because it was company-to-company, they had to include them.

Another client contract demanded we not only delete any data they sent us at the conclusion of services (a common, if rarely enforced, provision when dealing with proprietary information), but that we *physically destroy the equipment on which the files were stored* and provide proof. Additionally, any contacts we made during the course of production were to be considered confidential, and any communication after the contract would be a breach of NDA (so, attempting to friend someone on LinkedIn or Twitter that I got along well with was an absolute no-no). On the one hand, I get it: You want to protect your code from leaks and your people from being enticed by other studios. But they were so adamant and inflexible that I had to walk away on principle.

I mean…you're insisting I shred my hard drives because I have a spreadsheet template you sent me to write your barks? Are you kidding me?

So much of freelancing is spent mulling over what we should be asking for, if we're asking for too much, if we're asking for too little, etc. How do we keep from measuring our self-worth in terms of the rates we're able to get from clients?

Self-worth is a hard thing to gauge, and the parameters may change over time, but I believe the factors that dictate it should be internal rather than external. For many in our society, financial compensation for individual labor is the primary measure of success, as well as whether or not the business/profession is sustainable/profitable and, secondarily, whether one's basic human needs are met.

But there's no dollar amount I can put on the sense of fulfillment being a storyteller brings, and I'd like to believe that would be just as true regardless of if I were a pauper or a king.

That's a pleasing turn of phrase, and part of me means it, but seriously: Fuck capitalism and fuck monarchies.

We often think of how much we're going to be paid because that is something that causes freelancers stress, and it's something we talk (and rant) about a lot to each other. However, we can put a lot of energy into a project. How can we evaluate the other types of investments freelancers can make, like our time, emotional energy, etc., and whether a project is worth it based on those costs?

It's impossible to know whether a project will be worth the intangible investments until it either ships or sinks. Recently, I had two projects that I cared deeply about *and* had a high amount of authorial/creative input collapse underneath me, and I was emotionally devastated. I'm talking break-up levels of distress, and I'm not entirely sure I'm over them yet. These were concepts I believed in, poured my creative energy into without reserve, and supported in every way I could conceive of beyond just the narrative (community building, etc.). But when things went sour and I found I couldn't continue on, I was *wrecked*.

I've been lucky in my life that every project I've worked on has connected in some way, large or small, with my personality or interests, while also encouraging me to expand and deepen my understandings. Often, there are also new skills or tangible assets that are acquired over the course of the contribution…learning to capture and cut a cinematic trailer, for example, or new audio equipment in order to set up a temp VO (voice over) pipeline. That's useful, for sure, but the danger is becoming too emotionally invested in the work. It's a risk I try to be aware of. Still, it happens sometimes, and sometimes it results in a project I'm radiantly proud of (Metacritic score be damned), while others it turns into a crushing heartbreak. There's no way to attach a commercial amount to those feelings but, for me, they're why I write. I don't do this for the money.

Beyond money, time, and emotional investment, are there other factors that go into whether you'll pursue a project or not? What's most important to you?

The most important consideration for me is: Does this project present the possibility of making someone's life a little better, my own included? Will writing this bring someone an iota of joy? A laugh? A thrill? A tear? A different way to see the world around them? A moment of introspection? Our audiences trust us with their time and imaginations. If that answer seems like a yes, I'm all in.

IT DOES AND DOESN'T GET EASIER

Once you get a strategy for figuring out what your rates should be, you can eyeball a project and know how much you should ask for it. That's the easy part! The hard parts? Asking for that rate (you never know just how the client is going to respond). When to raise your rates. Saying no to a project because it doesn't pay enough. Assessing if you can afford to take on a job that can't pay your rates, but you really love the project.

Freelancers can spend days talking about rates to each other because the art of negotiating and getting what we want are things we're always trying to perfect.

EXERCISE

What Should Your Rates Be?

Figure out what your rates should be (hourly, daily, weekly, fixed) based on your education, work in the industry, etc.

What professional sources will you use to help you figure this out? (Professional organizations, employee salaries, etc.)

If you already have rates you're using with clients, re-evaluate them to see if it's time to raise them.

NOTES

1. Adapted from Toiya Kristen Finley, "Freelancing in Games: Narrative Mercenaries for Hire," in *The Advanced Game Narrative Toolbox*, edited by Tobias Heussner (Boca Raton: CRC Press, 2019), 179–201.
2. Adapted from Toiya Kristen Finley, "Freelancing in Games: Narrative Mercenaries for Hire," in *The Advanced Game Narrative Toolbox*, edited by Tobias Heussner (Boca Raton: CRC Press, 2019), 179–201.

CHAPTER 13

Developing and Maintaining Great Client Relationships (and What to Do About the Bad Ones)

Freelancers have no business without clients. In a healthy business, free-lancers will have a few repeat clients who return to them with work for new projects and clients whom they may only work with once or twice. Once you get the job, the work of developing a relationship with the client begins.

Here are a few pointers to keeping that relationship successful and productive, and what to do in the unfortunate event that the relationship gets rocky.

DOI: 10.1201/9781003199779-15

ALWAYS BE PROFESSIONAL

This goes without saying, but it's a good reminder—we should always be professional in our interactions with clients. Professionalism is a foundation of our business. We and our businesses need to be taken seriously, and professionalism is one way to remind our clients of this.

Professionalism is more than your attitude or demeanor. You hear or read the word "professional," you might think of business suits, brief cases, and law or accounting offices. But that's not the atmosphere you'll find in game dev. Go to a game conference or studio, and you'll see lots of jeans and T-shirts.

When games are so casual, how do you act professionally?

Know Your Own Worth

- This isn't just about money—this is valuing yourself, as well as your work. When you value yourself, you expect other people to value you, too. It's easier to ask people to respect your boundaries as a free-lancer when you know you're worth it.

- But this is also about money. Knowing your worth is understanding the value of your knowledge, expertise, and body of work so that you can assess what all of that is worth money-wise.

- You attract better clients (ones who value you and/or are willing to pay you more), and you're more likely to avoid scam artists and people who will try to manipulate you.

Prove You're Trustworthy

- You turn in work by the deadline (or ahead of the deadline)!

- You're on time. You don't miss meetings.

Treat Others with Respect

- You value your team members.

- You give your teammates space to speak. If you're in a place of leadership, it's *imperative* that you give everyone a chance to give their input, especially marginalized people who often get ignored or who don't feel comfortable speaking up because of the environments they've been in before.

- You consider others' ideas even though you might not agree with them at first.

- You're respectful when you disagree.

- You give credit to others. If it's someone else's idea, you make sure everyone knows it. You don't take someone else's idea and make everyone think it's your own. Do people steal others' ideas and not give them credit? *Waaaay* more often than you realize.

- The respect you show others extends to your online communications.

Be Honest

- When you disagree, you say something, even when you're the dissenting voice. The client and the team won't see you as being a contrarian just for the sake of it. You may notice something no one else does.

- You let your client know things that might be difficult to hear. Clients bring you on to a project because they trust your expertise. If there's a problem, you address it, instead of potentially letting it go into the game.

When you're professional, people just feel better about you and your work overall.

BEGINNING THE RELATIONSHIP

Later in this chapter, you'll find a section called "Beginning the Working Relationship." This section is "Beginning the Relationship" because your working relationship with a client is different than your relationship outside of that project. You may know someone for years before they have a gig that's perfect for you. Your client might be a good friend or an acquaintance. And you will continue to know that person *after* you work on a game with them.

So, think of the beginning of the relationship with any client as *when you first meet them*. When you first meet someone, do you know they're going to become a client? No, of course not. But you never, ever know. Which means that you always want to be professional in your networking, while you're being yourself.

Where You Meet…

Where you meet prospective clients will dictate how formal you are with them and what you share about yourself and/or your business. You can meet a prospective client *anywhere*, so it's always good to be prepared! This is as simple as getting into the mindset where you share a little about yourself and what you do.

Meeting in Person
Networking Events

The most obvious place you'd expect to meet prospective clients is at networking events. These could be professional game conferences, fan conventions, dinners and parties after conference hours, local game dev meetups, or meetups for game-adjacent industries.

These are the types of events where you're expected to network, so everyone comes ready to give a verbal spiel about themselves. This can feel a little awkward, being a walking résumé. Just know that after years of networking, there are thousands of veterans who still feel a little weird walking up to complete strangers and talking about themselves.

Non-Networking Events

I use "event" loosely here. The act of meeting a prospective client somewhere *is* the event. In other words, the "event" could happen while you're shopping for groceries. These opportunities can take you by surprise because neither you nor the prospective client is expecting it, unlike a networking event where you're looking for opportunities, and the client is looking to hire people.

Active listening is important in these situations. You don't want to go into "sell" mode, but if you're having an engaging conversation, and the individual brings up an interesting project that you know you can help with, you can make the transition into discussing what you do, your services, and how you might collaborate on the project.

ALWAYS HAVE SOME BUSINESS CARDS!

Make sure you're always carrying business cards with you. You have no idea when you might meet a prospective client. It could be a random encounter on the street! I've started conversations with people seated next to me on planes and at holiday parties when the last thing on my mind was networking or offering freelancing services.

However, because I always carry a stack of business cards with me, I was able to hand people my cards. If I hadn't, I probably wouldn't have talked to them again or known how to get in touch with them.

You never know when you'll run into an unexpected opportunity.

Meeting Online   Whether it's LinkedIn, Discord, Twitter, Facebook, or other social media sites, your interactions are going to be conversational (maybe even more so than at networking events).

Like in-person meetings, talking to a prospective client for the first time can either be intentional or accidental. If you've joined a group dedicated to game development, you're probably looking for posts about gigs, or you might post that you're looking for one.

In other instances, you might engage in a conversation about game development, game writing, or another game discipline that interests you.

In either case, always remember you're conversing in a public forum. Some people may already know you online or in real life, but you'll be making a first impression to a broader audience (and, in effect, introducing yourself to that audience). Practicing good netiquette is how you must always conduct yourself—you don't want to be remembered as being problematic, argumentative, or just an unpleasant personality to be around. People *will* remember awful behavior. And because devs who are responsible for hiring are online, they might witness the bad behavior, or someone who witnessed a person making a fool of themselves will report back to them.

On the flip side, if you participate in conversations with thoughtful comments, you'll be remembered for the *right* reasons. You don't even have to comment all the time. Contribute when you have something to contribute.

Meeting via Professional Communication, Like E-mail   Something that surprised me about the industry when I got started is how informal communications are, especially over e-mail. As someone who'd been submitting prose fiction since I was 14, I was used to a certain level of formality and structure to e-mails. They were always business-like in tone.

Most query e-mails I receive from devs are more conversational. That's not a bad thing—it's just an observation for anyone who's not used to communicating with developers.

Still, we should always maintain a level of professionalism. If e-mails are about business, keep your messages concise, clearly answer questions if you need to, and ask thoughtful questions if you need more information. This is not just for e-mails; you're going to be responding to prospective clients over direct messages (DMs), whether the platform is Facebook, Slack, Discord, Twitter, or Instagram. It can be really easy to fall into text speak and misspell words, so *proofread* your writing before you send it.

If someone posts a job listing, I like to tell them in the thread that I'm going to contact them via DM. On Facebook, if you're not friends, your message can get filtered in Messenger, and the prospective client may never see it. The DM is a better place to ask any questions you may have, share your experience and why you're interested in the job, and send a link to your portfolio or samples. Doing this in the thread can clutter up information, and the client may have to wade through many posts just like yours. If there is an overwhelming number of them, clients may not see some of them, and they may only wade through comments from the first couple of days if the post is really popular.

Pay attention to the instructions in the post. Social media may be casual, but you still have to follow the freakin' guidelines. Just because the post's on Twitter or Facebook doesn't mean the client wants you to reply with your portfolio there. They may state an e-mail or website address for applications.

Vetting Goes Both Ways

You'd expect that a prospective client will vet you, but vetting clients is imperative for freelancers. You want to know that clients are who they say they are and that they have integrity. What do clients research when looking into you, and what should you research before executing a contract with *them*?

Vetting is a process for both the client and freelancer. Photograph by raggio5.

The Client's Vetting and Hiring Process

An excellent sign that a prospective client is professional and someone you want to work with is the fact that they vet you. Don't take offense to someone wanting to check you out. They're trying to verify that you are who you say you are, and you can do everything that you claim. Why else do you have an online website, a LinkedIn profile, and social media accounts where you're visible online? You *want* people reviewing your work.

It's not the only indication, but prospective clients who vet candidates signify how serious they are about their game and bringing the right people on board. Always have in the back of your mind that the clients are investing money in the project. Whom they hire will either ensure their game succeeds, fails, or is merely *a'ight*.

What does the client's vetting process look like? This may have a number of steps. The client may not go through all of them, but they will definitely go through some of them. I present this list as someone who was vetted in these ways and as someone who has vetted freelancers herself (in no particular order):

- **Initializing research.** Whom does the client need to hire? Who needs to be on the development team? What will it cost to bring all of these devs on to the team, and does the client have the budget for it?

- **Asking for referrals.** The client asks friends and acquaintances if they know devs who'd be a good fit for the development team. Referrals are important because clients expect to receive reliable names, and the referral in itself is a verification. The friends or acquaintances might reach out to freelancers, or the prospective client may do it.

- **Searching for devs.** Clients do their own search for freelancers they can add to the team. Clients may do this in conjunction with asking for referrals. They can seek a variety of sources, including LinkedIn searches, Google searches, social media searches (especially when looking for artists and animators), game credit repositories to see who worked on similar games, and freelancing platforms. After coming up with a list of candidates, the client might reach out to some or all of them.

- **Publishing the job description.** Clients announce positions they're looking to fill and give some information about the game.

- **Reviewing queries and applications.** Clients review the responses to their job descriptions or direct queries to freelancers and start eliminating candidates.

- **Asking for tests/samples.** Clients may ask for additional samples from candidates they're interested in or require tests to help narrow the field.

- **Conducting an interview.** Toward the end of this process, clients may interview candidates to get a better sense of who they are.

- **Making a decision.** Clients decide whom they'll hire. All sorts of variables go into the ultimate decision, including the client's budget, input from anyone who's already on the team or investing in the project, the freelancer's personality, and any work the client has reviewed.

Vetting Prospective Clients

Do clients you're thinking of working with have an online presence? Do they have company websites? Twitter accounts? Can you find out more about their project by what you find online? Vetting clients lets you find out how legitimate they are. There are scammers out there. But on the positive side, you can get a sense of people's personalities and what's important to them. When you're in a collaborative partnership (and the independent contractor–client relationship *is* a partnership), you want to know that you're compatible. And don't feel like you're spying on someone or snooping around. Prospective clients are looking to invest their money in someone. They're looking up everybody, too. You'll find that they'll visit your online portfolio and your LinkedIn profile because they want to get a better sense of who you are and if *you're* for real.

Here's what your vetting process might look like:

- **Reaching out to your network.** Do you know anyone who knows the client (or do people you know know someone)? Anecdotes of direct experience working with someone are the strongest indicators of what it's like to work with that person or team. And you'll find that if there are any red flags, people will want you to know. If a client is great, they'll want to give you glowing reviews. There are also instances where people have changed over time—for better or worse. So, older anecdotes may no longer apply. The industry is small, and reputations spread. This is yet another reason why having a great networking community, and members of that community you can trust are fundamental to your life as a freelancer.

- **Vetting their work history.** Look over the prospective client's LinkedIn profile. Does how they've presented themselves to you match up with their work history and experience? Now, if they've never worked on a game before, their LinkedIn profile may have nothing to do with games, so this isn't necessarily a bad sign. What *could* be a bad sign is if they've bounced around several jobs in a short period of time. *Why* were they not at a job for very long? Have they worked at a company you can look up on a review site like Glassdoor? Were employees disgruntled at that company at a time the client worked there? That might give you a window into the type of work environment the client is used to.

- **Vetting their social media.** Scan their social media feeds. Not only will you get a sense of their work history, but you'll also get a feel for their personality and how they interact (or don't) with other people.

- **Reviewing other freelancers' comments.** If you're on a freelance website like Fiverr or Guru, these sites will allow freelancers and clients to leave feedback for each other. You can find out a lot about clients through what they say about their past working relationships. Are their comments nasty? Are they complimentary? Do they have a bunch of jobs that were never completed, which should make you ask *why* they weren't completed? What do the freelancers say about them? Are *they* complimentary? If they ran into problems, what were the issues?

- **Evaluating the project.** You want to always be able to evaluate the project, based upon its status. But you'll want to get a sense of the project to see if it's even something you want to be a part of. Is the job posted publicly? Do the client's descriptions of the job to you personally match what's public? If they're different, ask how the job may have changed. You can ask the prospective client for any materials that will help you get a better idea of the game. Naturally, if you've signed an NDA, the client will be able to share more internal documentation with you than if you haven't. Check out any public information about the project, whether that's in interviews, first looks, the project's website, or developer logs.

Keep in mind that you're not going to get a full picture of a person by vetting them, whether you discover awful or amazing things about them. Ultimately, when you and a legitimate prospective client agree to work with each other, you're both choosing to have faith that you're going to have a great, collaborative relationship.

HIRING ON THEIR BEHALF

Sometimes, you'll need to put your vetting skills to use on behalf of your client. You may evaluate other freelancers to bring onto a project or hire subcontractors, whom you'll assign work to. Remember to evaluate freelancers based on what the project and client require, not just your own opinion.

If you are assisting with the hiring process, make sure you're paid for this! It could be an extra milestone, or you're paid hourly.

Trust Your Intuition (It's Not Just a Cliché)!

If prospective clients seem like jerks in their communication, they're probably jerks—*period*. If you get warning signs that make you uncomfortable, RUN AWAY. You might need the money, but you don't need the misery. You don't want to be in a horrible situation where the work feels exhausting or torturous. Your work will probably suffer, and stress will wreck your health.[1]

BEGINNING THE WORKING RELATIONSHIP

You've either applied for a gig, or the prospective client has reached out to you. Make sure you ask enough questions about the project (including the work environment and the tools the team might be using) to get comfortable with it and your role within it. Once you know what the job requires and you know how much time and energy you'll be devoting to it, you'll be able to give the client an estimated time table and state your rate or fee. During this negotiating process, the client may give you a budget, which you base your rate for the job on. The client will agree to your ask or offer you another rate. (There are magical times when the client informs you that you're asking for too little and will give you *more* than what you're asking for!) If the rate the client offers is acceptable for what the job entails, perfect. Contact the client or keep the conversation going. If what the client is offering is laughable, don't waste your time. You *might* be able to talk them into raising their budget if it's a little less than what you believe is fair. But I've been contacted out of the blue and asked what I thought something would cost. I gave them an answer, and I never heard from them again.

Once the contract is signed, you want to establish your workflow and how you will be communicating with your client (and possibly other team members). Since you'll be in the onboarding process, it's going to take some time for you to adjust and get used to *this* particular client's way of doing things. Be patient with yourself, your client, and the team as you're getting used to a new work environment and new personalities. If you're confused about something or feel you're missing something to do your job properly, don't be afraid to say so. It's not your fault if you have to hear things a few times before you get it down. You don't want to be caught off guard. For example, there's a misunderstanding between you and the client about your tasks at the very start. You assume the client will send you assignments, but your client uploads them to a Drive folder every week. This can be the start of communication issues, which will delay your work and create frustration between you, the client, and potentially other members of the team who rely on your work. Everybody communicates differently, so the beginning of a working relationship is the beginning of learning how to communicate with the new people you're working with.

ESTABLISHING BOUNDARIES

An important part of your working relationship with your client is to establish boundaries. If you have a personal relationship with the client, you'll especially want to make sure that there is a clear line between your work relationship and your personal relationship. I'm not saying that you can't be friendly with that client, but you do need mental and physical (including online) spaces where you keep things professional and focused on the job.

Have Working Hours!

Being a freelancer gives you the flexibility to set your own working hours—it's one thing that makes freelancing so great. If you want to work late at night, you can. If you want to work a certain set of hours on Monday and a different set of hours on Wednesday, you can do that, too. However, just because you might have a flexible schedule doesn't mean that you need to be accessible to your client at all hours. Let your clients know when they can and can't get in touch with you.

As I mentioned earlier, you'll need to negotiate your schedule with your client. There are certain times you *must* be available, like for meetings or designated work sessions. But there are times outside of those designated times when you don't *have* to be available. You're *not* an employee. Be accommodating, but not over accommodating.

 INTERVIEW WITH ELIZABETH PERALTA

Elizabeth Peralta is a multidisciplinary artist and designer from New York City. Throughout her design career, she has worked in fashion, graphic design, education, and user experience, and now she is expanding to augmented reality filters. She currently teaches visual computing at the School of Visual Arts. In her artist practice, she enjoys exploring the multifacetedness of diasporic Caribbean identity.

What led you to pursue freelancing, instead of employment?

When I first graduated in 2017, I was told many times at interviews or by recruiters that I did not have enough experience. I had friends that would pull me on to projects because they knew I had a diverse skill set. That led me to become a freelancer. I enjoyed working on multiple projects and having a flexible schedule.

What would you say are the most important characteristics of a healthy freelancer–client relationship?

Boundaries! Letting your clients know when and how to contact you. I personally do not give out my phone number to clients anymore. This should all be in the contract. Always have a contract.

What early steps do you take to help develop that healthy relationship?

Treat your clients with respect and speak in a natural but respectful tone. I make sure to ask my clients many questions about what is expected to make sure we are on the same page.

Your friends have hired you on projects before. The industry being as small as it is, devs end up being hired by their friends all of the time. How do you establish a clear line between the working relationship and the friendship relationship?

I think honesty and transparency between friends regardless of the working relationship is key. Being the best friend you can be by being caring and responsible both in and out of the workplace. Having clear communication with friends is important, too.

How do you maintain a professional tone with your friends when you're working with them?

By having clear and open communication. There is also a time and place for jokes and more intimate conversation. You may find that during work hours, you leave certain conversations for another time outside of work.

Why is establishing boundaries with your clients so important? What are ways that they can overstep those boundaries? Do you have any egregious examples you can share?

Establishing boundaries with clients is important because not having boundaries may lead to a miserable work life and relationship. I've had clients not sign my contract but expect me to work, I've had clients call me at three in the morning asking for deliverables (we were also in the same time zone), I've had clients insult my work, and I've had clients not pay me on time. What I have described was my experience with one single client. They later asked to work with me again. I declined.

How do you get your clients to honor your boundaries?

Once my boundaries are crossed, I make that clear and I never work with them again.

Have you had to fire a client?

Unfortunately, I wasn't aware that I could fire a client. I have always felt obligated to continue working until the project was delivered.

Have you worked with the same clients more than once? How do you develop great relationships with repeat clients so that you want to keep working with each other?

I have worked with clients more than once. As long as they are respectful and pay me when they say they are going to pay me, I am happy to work with them. It's really about respect for me.

On Communication Platforms

On Slack and similar platforms, there are options to set hours when you're available (or active), when you're away, and when you're unavailable. There are also lurk modes when you appear away. If there are times of day when you don't want to receive messages or notifications, make sure you put this in your profile.

Discord has similar settings for online, busy, idle, and invisible (lurking). You can set your status to busy, idle, or invisible when you're unavailable. My personal preference is to stay in lurk mode (or invisible). It's how I've always navigated the Internet. I'm online *a lot*, and I'm in several of my clients' Discord servers or Slacks, so I tend to see new messages right when they pop up or shortly after they're written. If I'm working at that moment, I might respond right away or wait a few minutes. (It's always good to read something a few times to make sure you understand it. Internet communications breed *misreading* or not fully understanding the other person because these platforms are designed to communicate quickly, so we read quickly and gloss over meanings.) But there are some messages I'll leave for later because I'm not currently working on that particular project.

You also don't have to set your devices to receive notifications, or you can set your devices to receive notifications during certain hours. I don't receive phone notifications from certain platforms, and when I also get e-mails on my phone from those platforms, notifications are overkill.

Set Your Calendar

Your clients may use apps like Google Calendar. Block off times when you're busy or unavailable.

Boundaries Are a Protection

Setting up boundaries keeps a client from intentionally or unintentionally taking advantage of you, your time, and your energy. When you feel that you always have to respond to a client *right away* or you feel you have to be accommodating even when you're not really available, you'll get stressed out, and it will affect how you feel about your client and the project.

As a freelancer, also, you can take on as many or as few jobs as you want, as long as you can keep up with your commitments and turn in good work on time, and you don't overwork yourself. Limiting when your clients have access to you gives you the freedom to work more jobs at the same time, and even give you more time for yourself and your interests.

NEVER OVER COMMIT

None of us would ever say, "I'm going to do too much work!" But it happens. Freelancers over commit when they take on jobs beyond their skill sets, work outside of the scope of their contracts, or get extended beyond a reasonable timetable. Sometimes there's a desire to prove ourselves. What we don't realize is that when we get in this mindset, we can overextend ourselves, too. If we really like the client, we might agree to take on more tasks. If we haven't had a gig in a while, we might try to do anything to secure work. We might try to do a job we're not qualified to do,[2] even when the client believes we can.

When I was very young in my game writing and design career, I was hired to write for a children's game. This job was a Venn diagram of several of my backgrounds: I had written short fiction and nonfiction e-books to get kids interested in reading a couple of years before this gig, and I had a couple of game writing projects on my résumé now. The game was a platformer, and the clients didn't have a level designer. They asked if I would take on that responsibility. Now, there was nothing stated in my qualifications that suggested I could be a level designer. Sometimes, a client may not understand the differences between disciplines (this is a common occurrence on freelance platforms like Upwork, Fiverr, and Freelancer). Just because "game designer" and "level designer" have "designer" in their titles, that doesn't mean the roles are interchangeable.

Did I want to *try* my hand at level design? Sure. It was not something I would have considered before they asked. I started imagining what I would be doing as a level designer. Was that the time to experiment as a level designer for the first time and learn on the job? Absolutely not. I had no understanding of what being a level designer entailed. While I was curious, the idea that I would be a level designer on a project when I had no business being one filled me with dread.

So, why did I even consider it for the half second that I did? Well, I was still new to my game development career. To that point, people knew me as a writer (most people still think of me as a writer or narrative designer, and not a game designer). I wanted a chance to prove my versatility. After all, more versatility = more job opportunities. And this was a time in my life when I was getting very few jobs because I had very few opportunities, and I only knew of limited places to seek them out. But I let my clients know there was no way I could be a level designer. I had never been one, and I certainly hadn't developed the skills for what they needed. Instead, I explained to them why they needed someone with experience in level design—which they appreciated—and gave my opinion on level designers they were considering.

The other problem with over committing or trying to do work when we can't is that we hurt our relationships with our clients. If we're working too hard, everything we do suffers. If we try to take on responsibilities we're not qualified for, not only will we end up producing something we're not proud of, but we'll also set our clients' projects back, and we'll cost them time and money. They'll have to hire *someone else* to clean up our mess.

Relationships with honesty as part of their foundations are long-lasting ones built on trust. If your client's project timetable is too short, let them know. Don't try to get everything done in time you know you don't have. If your client's asking you to take on too much, let them know why you're unable to do what they're asking. If your client is asking you to wear more than one hat, and you *can* do that work, make sure they're paying you for both of those hats. Doing more than one job for only one price is a good way to overextend yourself, and you may come to resent the work and your client in the process.

It's important to note here that reasonable clients with integrity will understand why you're telling them no. A client that's looking to exploit you will tell you that *you're* the unreasonable one. That's a giant, flashing neon sign that that's not someone you want to be working with.

DEVELOPING A RAPPORT

Developing a rapport with people we work with happens naturally, but consider this a *strategy* for getting more comfortable in communicating with your client. The faster you understand how everyone communicates, the more effective you'll be.

 INTERVIEW WITH MITU KHANDAKER

Dr. Mitu Khandaker is a game designer, scholar, and entrepreneur. She is CEO and co-founder of Glow Up Games, a mobile free-to-play studio addressing the largest hidden audience in games: women of color. She is Assistant Arts Professor at the NYU Game Center, where she teaches game design and development. She holds a PhD on designing games for immersive interfaces such as VR, and has a background in computer engineering.

Mitu has launched games and tech start-ups previously, as well as working in the indie space. She has received a number of international accolades, including the Breakthrough Brit BAFTA in 2013. Mitu has served on the advisory committee for the Advocacy Track at the Game Developers Conference since 2014. She is also on the board of directors at Feminist Frequency, and is an AAAS IF/THEN Ambassador, promoting game development as a career path for girls.

Note: At the time of this interview, I was working with Glow Up Games as a freelancer.

A lot of developers are wary of working with telecommuting freelancers. Why do you believe that is?
I believe it's an issue of trust—and sometimes that is understandably so. It's no secret that game development budgets are usually pretty tight, and many projects are under-resourced and overscoped. So, if a developer does not feel confident that they'll be able to quickly establish a good working rhythm with a freelancer, it can be harder to justify.

So, in part, it's like *any* kind of relationship where trust has not already been established; sometimes that can be more difficult to do remotely rather than in person. However, trust is a two-way street: As much as it is up to freelancers to establish trust with a potential client, it is also up to the developers to extend that trust. Admittedly, it may mean that this takes extra work on the developers' part; for instance, getting freelancers onboarded onto a project can require more coordination and investment in time—but it's one that I believe can pay off significantly by increasing the size of your collaboration pool and, crucially, increasing the diversity of your project.

What advice would you give developers who are considering working with telecommuting freelancers, but they may not know how to integrate these freelancers into their teams?

Communication! Plus, setting clear boundaries and expectations. These are all just as important for any in-person teams, of course, but working with telecommuting freelancers underscores this importance even further. It is important to establish things like: What days and hours can you expect them to work on a regular basis, and when should they be considered reachable via any communication mediums like Slack or Discord? What are the clear deliverables you can expect from them, and what are the deadlines and expectations? How are they reporting any issues or updates about their work? These are all important in establishing trust with a freelancer.

There are also specific challenges depending on whether a telecommuting freelancer is joining a mostly in-person team, or if there are already a number of employees who are also telecommuting. When you're working in an in-person, colocated environment, sometimes there are ad hoc meetings that happen or decisions that get made, and this is particularly true in a fast-paced development environment. I think working with freelancers helps keep you honest about these types of things; are you involving all the appropriate stakeholders? Are decisions being documented appropriately? Sometimes, it may require more coordination, but this is important to the health of the team and the project.

Also, just as importantly, are you helping the freelancer feel, on an *emotional* level, like they are as much a part of the team as any in-person contributors? If there are in-person social events that telecommuting freelancers feel excluded from, that can be an issue, too. So, finding opportunities to host all-remote events, for instance, can be important!

How have you discovered the freelancers you've hired?

It's largely been a mix of word-of-mouth recommendations, and putting out calls on social media—especially Twitter. I cannot stress enough the importance of a Twitter presence for freelancers in the games industry!

What has been your experience working with telecommuting freelancers?

At Glow Up Games, we started as a mostly remote team—including the founders! So we were already set up to support the telecommuting format. This also meant that when the world went into lockdown for COVID-19, we were already prepared with an arsenal of remote working tools that we were used to, such as Slack and Zoom. Starting remotely gave us an opportunity to work with folks that we may not otherwise have been able to consider—and as a team specifically dedicated to making games for underrepresented players and also enacting structural change around *who* gets to make games, this was especially important for us.

What three pieces of advice would you give freelancers, as someone who hires them?

- A freelancer who over communicates is far better than one who under communicates! If you have questions, issues, or if you're struggling in any way, it's best to let your client know ahead of time—this is a behavior that goes a long way in establishing trust!
- Carve out regular time that you are available for work, if possible. Clients appreciate that transparency for their own planning purposes.
- You're an important part of the team as much as any employee may be!

HEARING YOUR CLIENTS' VOICES AND UNDERSTANDING THEIR PERSONALITIES

You'll want to develop a rapport with your new client as soon as possible, even if you're friends or acquaintances with that client because how you communicate with each other changes in a more professional setting. When you're comfortable with each other, it's easier to share ideas, ask tough questions, make tough decisions, and talk through disagreements.[3]

If it's technologically feasible, have a call over a platform like Zoom, Discord, etc., even if you spoke with them directly during your hiring process because your relationship changes once you're on the project. It's easier to see someone in three dimensions, not just words you read in an e-mail, on a Slack post, or a wiki article when you can hear their voice. You get a better feel for their personality and how they communicate when you can speak directly to them. You've probably read the advice that you should be careful with online communications because it's easy to misread the writer's tone and emotion. The opposite is true when you hear someone's voice—who they are in their writing becomes that much clearer when you can pair the voice and personality with the persona you read in their writing.

However, it *is* important to understand the other ways in which your clients (and your teammates) communicate, including through writing. You may have clients who communicate on a macro, broad-strokes level. They know those all-important details, but they might not always write them out. Once you understand that, you'll know that you simply need to ask clarifying questions to get those details. On the flip side, your client might be super detail oriented, but you need perspective on the bigger picture.

As I mentioned in Chapter 10, "The Online (?) Portfolio," everyone reads differently because our brains are all different. Figuring out how you need to structure your writing and organize your ideas to accommodate those learning styles will help you better serve your teammates, they learn how to process your ideas, and you become integrated into the team faster.

How Do You Like to Communicate?

I hate doing game dev stuff on Discord, Slack, and Skype. Hate, hate, *hate* it. In the past few years, these have become preferred means of communication. They're all too disorganized for my brain, especially when everyone posts really important information in channels, and it's not easy to sift through 60 messages to find the content that's relevant to what I need to do.

How you prefer to communicate is something else you'll need to address with your client. This doesn't mean that you'll be able to avoid using certain platforms or other forms of communication you don't enjoy but, as I've mentioned several times, everything should be a give and take. I might have to communicate on Discord or Slack, but I also have my own docs on Drive that the client can look over to answer some of my own questions. I make it clear that for really important conversations, I'll probably send an e-mail, so I can easily find information and back-and-forth responses. I can later archive those e-mail threads and find them for review.

BE HONEST, BUT RECOGNIZE WHEN THE FIGHT IS OVER

There will be times you and your client have disagreements. You'll want to dig in and win your client over to your point of view, especially when you're emotionally invested in the game. (When you don't care as much, you're more inclined to agree with whatever your client wants. Apologies to any clients reading this.)

The best you can do is to make your case as to why your argument is best for the vision of the game. Give as detailed information as you can, and if your teammates agree with you, that's great.

However, the client's always going to have the final say because they (or their investors) are putting all of the money into the project, and they're the ones paying you. If you and your client are stubborn, you don't want to get to a place where you strain your working relationship. When your client has made a final decision, it's time to stop trying to sway them, even if you think your client doesn't understand why you're making a suggestion or trying to steer them in another direction. I had a client who had never made a game before, and there was a lot he didn't understand about game development or different types of games. Our team would often clash with him because he lacked some of this knowledge. There were definitely fights we lost where we knew he didn't understand what we were advocating.

Recognize, too, that sometimes the final say is not with your client. They might agree with you. They might even fight on your behalf, but their publisher or investor(s) can override their decisions.

It's frustrating when your ideas are rejected or a client makes a decision that you know could hurt the game. Ultimately, remember that your client isn't rejecting you.

Who Makes the Final Decision?

If you're a subcontractor, or your contact on a project is an employee of the client, you're not in direct communication with the person who has the final say on any aspect of the game. This means that your contact may like your work, but they can't authorize your payments or put that final stamp of approval on the work you turn in.

Find out if you can get in contact with the final decision maker, so you're not always having to go through a third party who's not signing off on your work. Now, you may not always be able to talk directly with the decision maker. They may have set up their leadership hierarchy because they *don't* have to talk to you. Or they might be so busy that they put someone else in charge of the game, and they simply sign off on the project's direction. But, if you *can* get in touch with the one who has the final say, this can keep your work from continually being rejected if there's any miscommunication between what you think the client wants and what they actually want. Or you can unblock any delays because you can get clarification from the source, instead of waiting for your contact to get information from the client and reporting it back to you. (For more on this, please read Chapter 14, "Please Learn from My Ignorance.")

I subcontracted on a project where the client, the main freelancers, and I were all on the same forum, so I had direct access to the client. There were quite a few times when I needed clarification on an assignment. When the client provided an answer, I immediately had access to it and didn't have to wait for another freelancer to report it back to me. If I were not getting that information quickly, it would have delayed when I could have worked on my assignments. I had set aside that time because I had other gigs. Being delayed would have wrecked my schedule.

ENDING THE CLIENT RELATIONSHIP (INCLUDING FIRING YOUR CLIENT)

A lot of times, you'll work with a client once. With other clients, they may become repeat clients, and you may work on two, three, or more than ten games with them. But there may be times when you have to end relationships with clients for a number of reasons.

Ending Things Amicably

Sometimes, the relationship just doesn't work out, despite both you and your client trying to make it work. You might have creative differences you can't reconcile. Your work styles might clash. If you're noticing you're having a tough time working with your client, they probably have, too.

The worst-case scenario is that you have a client who doesn't respect you. They don't respect your boundaries. They're rude to you, or they're demanding. This is an environment you absolutely want to get out of. It will affect your physical and mental health and sour your relationship to your work. I say all of this knowing it can be an extremely difficult decision to leave a problematic project when you need money, and you're in the mindset that you'll take whatever you can get. (I'd been in that situation working with ITT.)

Sometimes, you'll be on the other side of the relationship ending, and it's the client who has to terminate the contract. I've been there, too. It's no fun to hear that your client is out of funding, and there's no place for you anymore. Or the publisher wants to go in a completely different direction. Or the money behind the game just doesn't want to support it anymore. When this happens, say that you understand (it happens way more than anyone would like), but you can be honest and admit you're sad to be leaving. Make sure you express wanting to work with the client again, whether they're at the same company on another project, or they move on someplace else.

Whether your relationship is good or rough, you want to end things as smoothly as possible. This will be good for your reputation. And in the case that you really came to like the project or the client, you can help them correct whatever's going wrong.

Understand Your Contract

All contracts should have clauses about the client or freelancer terminating the agreement. The language usually focuses on their being a mutual understanding for the parties to stop working together. This is how the clause reads in a free work-for-hire template available online[4]:

7. Termination of Work for Hire Agreement

As with most work for hire agreements, this contract may be terminated at any time by either the company or the contractor so long as the following conditions are met:

7.1 The resigning party provides the other party 30 days notice before terminating the contract.

7.2 In case the company is terminating the work for hire agreement, they shall pay the contractor all outstanding dues including the amounts that have accumulated up to the date of termination.

7.3 In the event of termination of the work for hire agreement, the contractor shall surrender all documents, work in progress, materials obtained and any other relevant paperwork before terminating the agreement. The contractor shall continue to be bound by the confidentiality clause contained in section 6 of this document.

This work for hire agreement is governed by the prevailing law of the land and has come into being for performing lawful works. Both the company and the contractor fully understand the terms and conditions listed in the document and agree to abide by them.

This particular contract mentions that one party gives the other a notice of 30 days, but this time frame can be shorter or longer. Based on what you negotiate with your client, you may or may not have to give a reason for wanting to terminate the agreement.

Be Honest about the Relationship

Explain what's going wrong and why you feel it's time for a change. Your client might want to try to work out any problems you're having. It's up to you whether you want to try for a trial period or end it immediately.

Offer Referrals

If it turns out you weren't the right fit, you can give the names and contact info of people who might be interested in the project. This illustrates that you did care about the project, and you want it to succeed. The client will also think well of you, and they will be more likely to offer your name as a referral in the future.

If Things Get Nasty…

If your client demands that you stay in a job when you don't want to (and you're not obligated to!), this can make your decision to leave a lot easier. Freelancers and clients end relationships all of the time. If they can't respect this, then this isn't a collaborative relationship you want to be in. Leaving might be painful, especially if the client is nasty about it.

Stay professional, and if you ever have to explain *why* you left the project, make sure you have evidence. A client might attempt to tarnish your reputation. Keep e-mails and take screenshots of their bad behavior. You'll want to take screenshots as soon as possible; you might get locked out of an account with no access to the messages if you wait.

You don't want to go around talking about how awful the client was. That will make prospective clients wonder about *you*, and worry that you might talk about them in the same way if they should work with you. However, if you ever have to defend yourself and someone asks you specifically about an experience or you need to protect yourself legally, this is when you'll have evidence of the facts.

New Rates and Loyal, Older Clients

Sometimes, you get too expensive for a client. There's no shame in this. It simply means that, in your career, you've gotten to a place where you're more respected, and you can ask for higher rates. That means that some of your repeat clients, ones that you may really enjoy working with, can no longer afford you. You might grandfather these clients in and keep them at your old rate, but you may have to move on from them. This can be a difficult decision, especially if you need money, and you have prospective clients who are ready and willing to pay you more.

You don't have to cut off an older client immediately. You can let them know that your rates are going up, but you will consider doing another job or two with them at your old rate. After that, they'll have to pay you at your higher rate. If they want to keep working with you, and they know they have upcoming projects that are perfect for you, this gives them time to acquire the funding needed to retain your services.

For more on how to announce your new rates to a client gracefully, see Shel Kahn's interview in Chapter 12, "Establishing Your Rates: The Eternal Freelancer Question."

"PROFESSIONAL" DOESN'T MEAN YOU CAN'T BE PERSONAL

I don't want this chapter to come across as if being professional means you have to drain all of the joy and fun out of the collaboration process. When you like and get along with your clients, your work will be better, and your work environment will be better for everyone. And you can absolutely consider your clients to be friends.

AND A GENTLE REMINDER…

I've left an important tip for having good relationships with your clients for last—you know that your client is *not* your employer. I'm going to harp on this. If you even unconsciously think of yourself as an employee, it will affect how you interact with your client, and this will change the power dynamics between you. You'll forget the rights you have as a freelancer, and you won't establish the necessary boundaries that will help to define the freelancer–client relationship.

When you *know* you're a freelancer, really understand that as part of who you are, you will establish those boundaries, and you'll be freer to express your opinion and introduce your ideas (and *fight* for those ideas).

EXERCISE
Where Are Your Business Cards?

You want to have your business cards on you at all times. You never know when you're going to begin a relationship with someone who could be a future client. If you don't already carry your business cards everywhere, find a place to put them so that they'll always be on you. I carry my business cards in one of my backpack pockets.

Where can your cards go, so you'll have easy access when you need to grab one?

NOTES

1. Adapted from Toiya Kristen Finley, "Freelancing in Games: Narrative Mercenaries for Hire," in *The Advanced Game Narrative Toolbox*, edited by Tobias Heussner (Boca Raton: CRC Press, 2019), 179–201.
2. This is a *very* different situation than a job we haven't done before. *Everybody* has a job they've never done before once. Say you're a game writer, and you take on a narrative designer role for the first time. You have all of the skills and insight to be a narrative designer, but this is your first opportunity. The same is true when you start taking on more senior roles.
3. And any development cycle can be full of disagreements—simply because the publisher wants changes, you run into a technical issue, or your funding unexpectedly becomes limited—and you have to work around these new parameters.
4. "Work for Hire Agreement," LAWS, last modified December 23, 2019, https://doc.laws.com/work-for-hire-agreement.

CHAPTER 14

Please Learn from My Ignorance

It's only fair to share some horror stories with you, of what *could* happen with clients if you don't have guardrails in place, or you're skipping over little details that could fortify your business. Why would I say that? Freelancers can have some harrowing experiences. I hope you never have to deal with fraudulent clients, difficult clients, or payment situations where you remain…unpaid. These are just a taste of the unique (and uniquely wacky) situations you may find yourself in. I look back at them now and think, *Good God, I lived through that?* Each experience made me a bit savvier and taught me that there were protections and practices I hadn't built in to my contracts, or that I needed to better understand the leadership hierarchy on all of my projects, or that there were little things I could do at home to keep my work safe. Unfortunately, going through these types of things is a major way you learn what you need to change about your business practices.

For your amusement, here are some nuggets of wisdom I had to learn the hard way. May similar scenarios never befall you. And may "Please learn from my ignorance" be a refrain that rattles around in your mind

DOI: 10.1201/9781003199779-16

whenever you take on a new job or find yourself needing to finesse a tough situation.

BACK IT ALLLLL UP

During the Facebook social games craze, I was working on a project as both the game designer and the narrative designer. The game design document (GDD) I was writing was due that night.

Now, I'm the type who hits [CTRL] + [S], like, after I type anything new into the document to save it. And I have an external hard drive to back up all of my documents. At this point in time, however, I had not backed up my docs in a couple of days. Why? I don't know. Was I too busy to save everything? Anyway, I figured I would back everything up once I sent off the GDD.

You already know where this is headed.

Just as I was finishing up this 50-something-paged doc, my old, reliable version of Word decided to crap out on me. And it not only was on the verge of crashing, it was also the type of total train wreck that, when I tried to save the GDD, Word was creating a corrupted file that was overwriting my nearly completed document. The only way to fix what was happening was to reboot my laptop—which meant I was going to lose all of my GDD.

I was in full panic mode. I e-mailed my client to let them know what was happening. I remember explaining to my mother that everything was pretty much hopeless. On a last-ditched whim, I copied the entire document and pasted it into a Google Drive document.

I shut down my computer, expecting the worst.

I opened Word. Totally borked, unreadable GDD.

I went to Drive…

…and there was that GDD, copied and pasted in its totality.

I was shaking. I realized how close I'd come to losing weeks of work, simply for not backing the doc up on my external hard drive or keeping another copy on Drive. I remember as I sat at my desk with my head in my hands, I felt my mother wrap her arms around my neck and hug me from behind.

The formatting was somewhat of a mess, but I downloaded the doc and quickly made corrections. Then I e-mailed the client with something along the lines of, "Never mind. Everything's fine, lol.[1] By the way, here's the GDD."

Back up your work. Back it *allllll* the way up.

And please learn from my ignorance.

THE POWER OF "NO"

I've said it before. I'll say it again—as a freelancer you are *not* an employee. You are your own boss. You are in a collaborative, business relationship with your client. You're working *with* your client, not *for* them. Your client is not your employer.

That means that you can tell your client "**no**."

Let me say it again: You can tell your client "**no**."

I knew this, but didn't *really* know it yet with one of my clients. Back in my Elance days, I had done one project with him and he liked my work and asked me to be a part of another project. I agreed. At one point, he asked me to write a particular document I'd never done before.

An inner panic set in. I understood that there was an art to this type of doc, it wasn't creative writing, and I didn't have those skills. I expressed my concerns and told him, "I've never written this before."

"You can do it!" he said.

Okay. My thought process was basically this: He was a repeat client, I wanted to keep him as a repeat client, and I would get the chance to learn some new skills that I would probably use again.

So, we agreed that I would deliver the assignment in two weeks. I did research and analyzed a few examples, and I turned it in.

He hated it. Not only did he hate it, but he basically flamed me when he rated me and left a review on Elance. Basically, he said, I didn't want to do the job, and I had wasted his time.

Whew! Chile! That was…*something*. I waited a bit and gathered myself before I said anything, so I would not respond to his review in kind.

As graciously as I possibly could in my response to that review, I pointed out that I'd done what was asked of me, and he had left quite a glowing review for my last project with him…which anyone could see in my review history.

And then I messaged him, let him know he had not paid me for the work, and made sure he paid me for my work.

What if I had quite firmly said **NO** to the assignment? Sure, I may have lost a client, and I may have been out of a few hundred dollars. Would losing that client have been such a bad thing? He proved himself to be someone I didn't want to work with again anyway. And his comments could have hurt my work prospects. Thankfully, that didn't happen.

Speaking plainly about what you do and don't want can lose you opportunities, but it can also save you a lot of stress (and potential hits to your reputation).

Please learn from my ignorance.

OUT-SCHEME THE SCAMMER[2]

My client was a developer of social games, and they hired me as a subcontractor. I was not in contact with the developer's clients on one game when the developer had subcontracted work out to me. It was very difficult trying to understand what the client wanted because they didn't play games. Basically, this was the era of Facebook games, and they wanted to make a clone of an extremely popular game on the platform at the time. The project manager and I discussed among ourselves why it would be a good idea to add *some* originality to the game. He took my concerns to the clients, but we were still getting vague answers. Honestly, I don't know specifically what the clients were saying or how the project manager was conveying my concerns. I never saw any written communication between them or talked to the clients directly. Now, you might be thinking, *Gee, Toiya, sounds a little shady.* Hold that thought…

The project manager and I decided that I would write up a list of questions about the clients' audience, the game's genre, games that were similar to the one they wanted to develop, etc. When I got the questionnaire back, I saw that only two or three of the questions were answered…out of, like, ten. Communicating with the client was difficult enough. It was even more frustrating when I had to do it through the project manager.

What would have been *awesome* is if I had insisted on speaking directly with the clients. I could have explained why the questionnaire was important. (Actually, I probably wouldn't have needed the questionnaire because I could have talked them through a decision-making process.) However, because the developer had a pretty haphazard way of doing things, I was never going to be able to speak with the clients, even if I requested it.

On the other hand, on my next (and last) project with this developer, I *was* in contact with their client. In fact, we had weekly meetings. Why could I speak directly with this client and not the others? As I said, the way this developer operated did not make sense.

Being in contact with my client's client worked to my advantage when the developer refused to pay me. I got the project through Elance. We had agreed I would be paid via milestones, but the developer put the total amount into one payment that I would get once the project was completed. I put in a request to have more milestones set up, not realizing that the system would erase the one existing milestone and send the money that had been put into escrow back to the developer's account. Throughout my time on the project, I kept reminding the developer to create the milestones and put the money in escrow. All the while, I was pretty sure the developer was going to try to screw me over. And, of course, that's exactly what they tried to do once I finished my part of the project.

I had one major advantage: Per Elance's contract, all rights belonged to the freelancer until the client paid for the work. So, in not paying me, my client set up a situation where I owned all the work I had written on behalf of their client. Genius, no?

I went straight to the people who were having the game made and explained, "I own the content to everything I wrote for you until the developer pays me." They pressured the developer on my behalf, and I got a lawyer involved. I would have never heard from the developer otherwise and lost out on a significant amount of money if I had not been in contact with their client.

If you're subcontracting, find a way to be in contact with your client's client.

Please learn from my ignorance.

THE GHOSTS OF UNPAID PROJECTS PAST[3]

Some writing-related work I did for a very large AAA publisher only took about a month. It was a lot of fun, and I enjoyed working with the producer...

...and then the money didn't come. I asked the producer about it. He inquired on my behalf...

...and then I never heard back from him. So, I kept asking where my money was, and then I finally got an answer from the new producer working on the project. This was about six months later. He made some inquiries. Nothing happened. I wasn't near the offices, so I couldn't drop by and do the running back and forth, dealing with the red tape that I needed to get an answer. Finally, about a year and a half later, the second producer learned why I hadn't been paid: The company didn't have my bank account information to transfer the money.

Such a simple little thing. Just my bank account info! But the first producer didn't know to ask me for this when negotiating the contract because he wasn't in the habit of paying people. And at that point in time, I didn't know to ask how I would be paid and what information they would need from me. *A year and a half.* Did I mention this was during one of my lean periods, and I really needed that money right after I finished the project?

Please, y'all, *please.* Learn from my ignorance.

NOTES

1. Okay, it didn't read somewhat like this, but that's how I felt.
2. Adapted from Toiya Kristen Finley, "Freelancing in Games: Narrative Mercenaries for Hire," in *The Advanced Game Narrative Toolbox*, edited by Tobias Heussner (Boca Raton: CRC Press, 2019), 179–201.
3. Adapted from Toiya Kristen Finley, "Freelancing in Games: Narrative Mercenaries for Hire," in *The Advanced Game Narrative Toolbox*, edited by Tobias Heussner (Boca Raton: CRC Press, 2019), 179–201.

CHAPTER 15

Some Final Thoughts

I MENTIONED WAY BACK IN Part I that I didn't know working in games was something I could do. This isn't unusual in the Black community in the United States. There are kids who would probably want to work in games if they knew it was a viable career path. A few years before my mother retired, when she worked with kids who were into games, she would tell them, "My daughter works in games. Did you know you could work in games?" A light would come on inside of them. For one of these students, his teacher started researching game engines when she saw how interested he was. He and a friend got time to pursue making games as a reward for good behavior.

For the most part, though, Black kids don't know about this world because their teachers, parents, and guidance counselors don't know to tell them about it. They're not seeing people like themselves working in games, either.

The first few years I went to GDC, people were trying to give me what they considered helpful advice: Want to be successful in games?

Move.

I told you how taken aback I was by that. I did not want to move. It was incomprehensible to me.

"Move" might sound like harmless advice, but it can be an earth-shattering thing to hear for a marginalized person. And speaking as a marginalized person, I did not want to leave my family. I did not want to leave my friends. I did not want to leave my community and my support system.

DOI: 10.1201/9781003199779-17

233

One's family by blood or by choice is often the backbone for marginalized individuals. We know where we're safe, physically and emotionally. We know whom we can count on for emotional support, and sometimes that support *is* physical, if and when we're threatened. Some are not able to relocate and travel to and from an office every day because of medical conditions. It's also not feasible for a lot of marginalized people, especially BIPOC individuals, to leave their lives behind and move to some of the most expensive cities in the world. We just don't have the money for that.

And why should we when we can telecommute?

There are now more calls for diversity and inclusion all over the industry. Good. Great. Needed. Necessary.

Now, do more to prove it, those in positions of leadership. There are plenty of marginalized people *on this planet* who have the talent to work in games, but they can't because that would force them to relocate, it's impossible for financial reasons because it would uproot them from their support systems, or both. If developers do *not* make space for more marginalized people and meet them where they are, then it is turning away creativity, innovation, and new perspectives that could energize their games.

But what do I know?

I'm just a marginalized chick who didn't take the advice to move, and I seemed to have turned out okay.

Index

For Product Safety Concerns and Information please contact our
EU representative GPSR@taylorandfrancis.com Taylor & Francis
Verlag GmbH, Kaufingerstraße 24, 80331 München, Germany